The Pocket Scroll® Series

SHAAR PRESS

RABBI ABRAHAM J. TWERSKI, M.D.

TWERSKI *on* MACHZOR

ROSH HASHANAH

published by

PocketScroll®

SHAAR PRESS

Table of Contents

Ha Melech —
The King

The Days of Awe

The ten days comprising the period of Rosh Hashanah through Yom Kippur are generally referred to as *Yamim Noraim*, the Days of Awe. The Torah literature states that these are days of judgment, when Hashem weighs our actions during the past year and ordains the course of our lives for the coming year.

Because of the fateful character of these awesome days, it is customary for the preceding month, Elul, to be a time of introspection, when we take detailed inventory of what we did and did not do in the preceding year.

The principle of the Days of Awe is summed up in the closing prayer of Yom Kippur, with the following words, "Say to them, 'As I live — the words of Hashem — I do not desire the death of the wicked one, but rather the wicked one's return from his way that he may live'" (*Ezekiel* 33:11).

Living according to the mitzvos of the Torah does not benefit Hashem. "If you are righteous, how do you benefit Him? Indeed, what has He taken from your hand?" (*Job* 35:7). The mitzvos were given to us for our benefit, and if we transgress them, it is to our own detriment and we are the ones who are harmed.

The medical profession warns us that cigarette smoking is a leading cause of cancer. If an individual is so foolish as to disregard the warning and subsequently develops cancer, the doctor may do his utmost to treat it, but he cannot undo the damage caused by the person's actions. Not so with Hashem, Who warns us not to deviate from the Torah; yet if we do, He gives us the opportunity to repent (do *teshuvah*), and if we do so sincerely, Hashem undoes the negative consequences of our own actions.

There are many dangerous lifestyles that one may indulge in with disastrous physical and mental consequences. Imagine how thrilled a person who suffers as the result of reckless behaviors would be if, when he confesses to the doctor how foolish he was, the doctor would wave a magic wand over him and undo all the damage! There is a "magic wand" that can undo the spiritual damage of deviating from the Torah: *teshuvah!* But Hashem does not wield that magic wand: we do! If we utilize it properly, He will restore us to spiritual health.

Teshuvah is powerful and effective all year round, but the *Yamim Noraim* are a particularly propitious time to ask for Hashem's acceptance of our *teshuvah*. To facilitate our *teshuvah*, the Sages composed appropriate prayers for the awesome days; these prayers are found in the *machzorim* (prayer books) for Rosh Hashanah and Yom Kippur.

The purpose of this volume is to provide greater understanding of some of the more prominent prayers in the *machzor*, in order to make the prayers more meaningful and to intensify one's *kavannah* (concentration, intent). One's *davening* (praying) in this manner will *iy"H* (if Hashem wills it) bring us to true *teshuvah* that will be joyously accepted on High.

May Hashem accept your prayers, fulfill all the desires of your heart for the good, and bless us with long life, good health, much *nachas*, and success in all that we do.

Kingship

*D*emocracy has taken its toll on our level of *yiras Shamayim* (awe of Hashem). In the Torah and in Talmudic literature we often find parables that seek to enhance our *yiras Shamayim* by relating, "If one were in the presence of a mortal king, how cautious one would be with one's words and deeds. How much greater should one's caution be in the presence of the Almighty King."

> *Rabbi Lipa Geldwerth tells of a man who came before his king to petition him for something he desperately needed. He was so frightened — overcome with the awareness of his king's majesty and with the knowledge that this king held the power of life and death in his hands — that he could not utter one word*
>
> *The king who was in a benevolent mood spoke kindly to the man, "Tell me what you need and I'll grant your desire." But the man was trembling so that he could not even open his mouth and he left the king's presence emptyhanded.*

Who nowadays can conceive of this combined feeling of awe and fear for a human king? This may not have much impact on us, since we do not relate to a mortal king. We elect a president for a period of time, and he does not have unrestrained powers. To the contrary, his powers are limited by congress and the courts. Once his term in office has ended, he is once again an ordinary citizen. Even in countries that do have a king, it is usually a ceremonial position, with power resting in the hands of an elected government.

Compare that with the Talmudical account of R' Yochanan ben Zakkai, whose disciples visited him when he was ill, and found him weeping. They said, "Light of Israel, the pillar of right, why are you crying?" R' Yochanan replied, "If I was being led to trial before an earthly king, who is here today but in his grave tomorrow, who, if he is angry with me, his anger is not eternal, who, if he imprisons me, the imprisonment is not eternal, who, if he puts me to death, my death is not eternal, and I am able to appease him with words or bribe him with money, yet I would be fearful and cry. And now, that I will be led before the King of kings, the Holy One, Blessed is He, Whose life and existence is eternal, and if He is angry with me, his anger is eternal, and if He imprisons me, the imprisonment is eternal, and if He puts me to death, my death is eternal, and I cannot appease Him with words nor bribe Him with money, shall I not cry?"

The disciples then asked him, "Our teacher, bless us." R' Yochanan replied, "May your fear of Hashem be as great as your fear of mortals." The disciples said, "Is that all you can say to us?" R' Yochanan replied, "I wish that it were so. You must know, when a person commits a sin, he reasons, 'I just don't want a person to see me (but is not concerned that Hashem sees him).'"

Shortly before his passing, R' Yochanan said, "Remove all the utensils so that they shall not become *tamei* (ritually contaminated) when I die, and prepare a chair for Hizkiyahu, king of Judah, who is coming to escort me" (*Berachos* 28b).

This interchange between R' Yochanan and his disciples is most enlightening. We believe Hashem exists and is All-powerful, but this belief is an abstraction, and may not be enough to deter a person from sin. If we have the emotional experience of the awe we have standing before a powerful earthly monarch, we may perhaps be able to extrapolate and develop the awe of standing before Hashem, the King of kings. But in a democratic country, where one may freely criticize the president or the ceremonial king, this reference point is lacking. R' Yochanan tells us that without this reference point, we may be remiss in awe of Hashem. We do not know what it means to tremble before a king.

Hashem said, "Recite verses of kingship before Me, to enthrone Me over you...and with what? With the shofar" (*Rosh Hashanah* 34b). The prophet says, "If the shofar is sounded in a town, will the people not tremble?. . .When a lion roars, who does not fear?" (*Amos* 3:6-8).

R' Yeruchem Levovitz of Mir said, "When I saw a lion, I understood its enormous might, and that as king of the beasts, all animals are in awe of him. Primitive peoples, seeing the might of the sun, worshiped it as a god, not realizing that the sun is but one of His many servants" (*Daas Chochmah Umussar* Vol.4 p. 248). In our *tefillos* we pray, "Let everything with a life's breath in its nostrils proclaim, 'Hashem, the God of Israel, is King, and His Kingship rules over everything.'" In our poverty of having an emotional experience of the awe of Hashem, we must extrapolate from objects that inspire us with awe, as a reference point for awe of Hashem.

"If the shofar is sounded in a town, will the people not tremble?" Beginning with the first day of Elul, we sound the shofar daily to inspire us with the awe of Hashem, that His Sovereignty is absolute. We must know that He controls everything in the universe, from the greatest galaxies to the most minuscule insects. The only thing that Hashem does not control is a person's moral decisions, because He has given a person freedom to choose between right and wrong."

It is of interest that when Rosh Hashanah occurs on Shabbos, we do not blow the shofar. This is not only to avoid a person's carrying the shofar in a public thoroughfare, but also because the *kedushah* of Shabbos, and the awareness that Hashem created the world and is its only Master, can provide the appreciation of Hashem's sovereignty. On Rosh Hashanah we say, "Today is the birthday of the world." Shabbos, like Rosh Hashanah, is a testimony to Hashem's creation of the world.

Belief in the existence of Hashem is not yet *malchus*. Primitive peoples believed in the existence of God, but felt that God was too supreme to bother with this tiny speck of the Earth and with mere mortals. That is why, in our *tefillos* of *malchus* we pray, "Reign over the entire universe in Your glory...Let everything that has been made know that You are its Maker." The Israelites, upon their liberation from Egypt, did believe in Hashem (*Exodus* 4:31), but it was not until they witnessed the miraculous dividing of the Reed Sea that they exclaimed, "Hashem shall reign for all eternity!" (ibid. 15:18). Only then were they convinced that Hashem controls the world and His Providence is over all things, animate and inanimate. This is why on Rosh Hashanah we begin saying *HaMelech HaKadosh*. Kedushah means that Hashem is separated and far above everything in the universe, but He is also the *Melech*, the King Who operates and controls the universe.

When we think of the infinite greatness of Hashem, and that by comparison we are less than infinitesimally small, we may lose our sense of significance. We must be aware that as creations of Hashem, we are endowed with a Divine soul, which makes us potentially great. This is why R' Yochanan, having expressed his utter effacement before Hashem, nevertheless told his disciples before his death. "Prepare a chair for Hizkiyahu, king of Judah, who is coming to escort me." He knew that no less a personage than Hizkiyahu, king of Judah, would greet him.

Every day, we cite many *berachos* and say, "Blessed are You, Hashem, Our God, King of the world." But precisely because we say these words so often, we do not concentrate on their meaning. Rosh Hashanah should give us a much greater appreciation of *malchus*, so that when we say the words, "Hashem, Our God, King of the world," we will think of Hashem's absolute sovereignty, and approach Him with the awe, the fear, and the respect that are His due.

It is customary that the reader of *Pesukei D'Zimrah* leaves the lectern before *HaMelech*. The *chazzan* then begins chanting *HaMelech* with its traditional tune in his place, then walks to the lectern to continue the services.

This practice is mentioned in *Aruch Hashulchan* (584), but no reason is given for it. My association is based on what I witnessed in a courtroom, when the judge said, "Let the defendant approach the bench." The defendant then walked humbly to stand before the judge. Perhaps the above practice conveys this ideal. The *chazzan*, representing the assembled, "approaches the bench" to stand before the Almighty Judge.

> *R' Ahron of Karlin began to chant the main portion of Shacharis, and when he pronounced the word "HaMelech," he fainted. When he was revived, he explained, "When I said 'HaMelech,' I was reminded of a story found in the Talmud regarding the period when the Romans laid siege to Jerusalem. R' Yochanan ben Zakkai — who was the leader of the Jews — lay down in a coffin, and pretending to have died arranged to have himself smuggled out of Jerusalem. Once outside the city walls, he came and stood before the general, Vespasian, whom he addressed as "melech" (king, emperor).*
>
> *"Vespasian said, 'I am a general. I am not the emperor.'*
>
> *"R' Yochanan said, 'There is no doubt that you are indeed the emperor. Scripture says that Jerusalem will fall before a king' (Isaiah 10:34).*
>
> *"At that moment, a messenger arrived from Rome. He informed Vespasian that the emperor had died, and that the Roman senate had appointed the general to be the new emperor.*
>
> *"Vespasian then said to R' Yochanan, 'If you knew that I was the emperor, why have you not come before me until now?'"*

R' Ahron continued, "When I said the word 'HaMelech,' I realized that Hashem may be saying to me, 'If you recognize Me as King, why have you not come before Me until now?'"

The great *tzaddik*, R' Ahron, who was totally devoted to Hashem, felt that he was derelict in not continually feeling as if he were in the immediate presence of Hashem. What can we say about ourselves?

R' Yisrael Salanter was sitting with a group of people and heaved a great sigh. Someone asked him if he was not feeling well.

R' Yisrael replied, "I happened to notice that the sleeve of my jacket is frayed, and I was embarrassed. Then I realized, if I am embarrassed in front of people because there is a defect in my jacket, how will I feel when I have to stand before Hashem, with all the defects in my mitzvos? That is why I sighed."

There are several insertions in the *Amidah* of the High Holy Days, which, if omitted, do not mandate repetition of the prayer. However, the modification of the *Amidah* that instructs us to refer to Hashem as "the Holy King" instead of as "the Holy God" is essential, and if one mistakenly said "the Holy God" instead of "the Holy King," the entire *Amidah* must be repeated.

The theme of the Divine Kingship permeates all the High Holy Days prayers. Even when we relate to Hashem as children to a loving father, we say, "Avinu Malkenu" — our Father, our King, not simply, "our Father."

Indeed, Hashem is a loving Father. I am reminded of the rabbi who wished to impress upon the congregation the magnitude of Hashem's merciful forgiveness. Standing before his congregants, he lifted his sweet, beautiful, 3-year-old son, and said, "Can anyone imagine this child doing anything that I would not forgive? It seems inconceivable, but if this sweet, beautiful child were to run into the street to retrieve his ball, I, his father, would soundly discipline him to make sure that he does not foolishly endanger himself again."

We must think of Hashem as a King Who issues commands to protect us from endangering our soul, Who promulgates decrees that determine the course of our lives for the coming year, and Who will pardon our sins when we do the requisite *teshuvah*.

The prophet says, "Seek Hashem when He can be found, call upon Him when He is near" (*Isaiah* 55:6). The Talmud says that this refers to the period from Rosh Hashanah through Yom Kippur, when Hashem, as it were, makes Himself more easily approachable to us.

R' Simchah Bunim of Pshische asked his young student, R' Mendel (who subsequently became the Rebbe of Kotzk), "Young man, where is God?"

R' Mendel said, "Everywhere. The universe is full of His glory."

R' Simchah Bunim persisted, "But, young man, I asked you, where is God?"

The bewildered R' Mendel said, "If my answer is not adequate, then please tell me."

R' Simchah Bunim said, "God is wherever one permits Him to be."

What R' Simchah Bunim meant is that a person may behave in a manner that repels God's Presence. "One with haughty eyes and an expansive [conceited] heart, him I cannot bear" (*Psalms* 101:5). The Talmud quotes Hashem as saying, "A vain person and I cannot exist in the same world" (*Arachin* 15b).

Chassidic writings relate that when the king is in his palace, it is difficult to obtain an audience with him. However, when the king goes among the people, he is more readily accessible. During the High Holy Days period, Hashem is closer to us. We must be humble and divest ourselves of the egocentricity and vanity that would erect a barrier between Him and us.

Hashem is indeed *Avinu Malkeinu*, both our Father and our King, and we dare not lose awareness of this boon.

Tefillah

The translation of *tefillah* as "prayer" leaves much to be desired. The dictionary definition of "prayer" is "a humble and sincere request, as to God." A request to Hashem is indeed one aspect of *tefillah*, but there are also several other aspects to *tefillah*, such as praise of Hashem, gratitude to Hashem, and yes, even complaining to Hashem.

At a gathering of Holocaust survivors, one woman, the
sole survivor of a family of eight children, said, "I go to
shul every Shabbos, but I don't daven. I sit there silently
in protest. I want God to see that I refuse to pray to
Him, because He allowed my family to be wiped out."

I could not but admire this woman's silent prayer and her profound faith. First, she has a strong belief in the existence of God
and is sure that He is All-powerful. If she did not believe this, she
would have no grounds for being angry with Him. Secondly, she
believes that He is immanently present in shul. I am not certain
that many people who do pray have such firm faith.

In what way can her silent protest be a *tefillah*? Some say that
the root of the word *tefillah* is related to the source for "bonding"
(Rashi, *Genesis* 30:8); i.e., *tefillah* is a process whereby one seeks to
come close to and to bond with Hashem. *Tefillah* is thus a relationship, and one can relate to Hashem by making a request of Him,
by thanking Him, by praising Him, and even by being angry *r"l*,
(God forbid), at Him. These are all ways of relating to Him.

There is nothing inherently wrong with grumbling to Hashem.
We find this fairly often in the immortal words of King David.
"Why, Hashem, do You stand aloof, do You conceal Yourself in
times of distress?" (*Psalms* 10:1). "My God, my God, why have
You forsaken me?" (ibid. 22:2). "Awaken, why do You seem to
sleep, O Lord?" (ibid. 44:24).

It has been said that Torah is Hashem speaking to man, and
tefillah is man speaking to Hashem. Hence, praying connotes a
relationship.

This answers the question, *Why is tefillah a mitzvah?* If I ask someone to help me, is that a mitzvah? The answer is that asking for Hashem's help is a means of relating to Him, and creating that relationship is the mitzvah of *tefillah*, regardless of the manner in which it is done.

The mere recitation of words without feeling is symptomatic of a very weak relationship. *Kavannah* (concentration, intent) is a necessary component of *tefillah*. Abarbanel expresses it very acutely: "*Tefillah* without *kavannah* is like a body without spirit"; i.e., it is lifeless (commentary to *Ethics of the Fathers* 2:13). Unfortunately, prayer is often recited by rote; we verbalize words while our thoughts are elsewhere. In his introductory prayer, "*Tefillah Before Tefillah*," R' Elimelech of Lizhensk laments, "Our thoughts are distracted even when we plead for our very lives."

On the other hand, *kavannah* can be very powerful even in the absence of formal prayer.

> *In the shul of the Chassidic master, R' Levi Yitzchak of Berditchev, the sounding of the shofar was delayed. R' Levi Yitzchak explained:*
>
> *"This morning, when people were streaming to shul, there was a lad, an orphan, who had not been given a Jewish education. When he saw everyone going to pray, he was envious and was overwhelmed with sadness because he had not been taught to read Hebrew. He said, 'Master of the universe. I do not know how to read the prayers. I know only the letters of the alef-beis, so I will say the letters, and You, God, put them together to form the proper words.'*
>
> *"We must delay the sounding of the shofar, because Hashem is now occupied with putting the letters together."*

We can imagine what *kavannah* this aroused.

Kavannah is essential in our *tefillah* all year round, but how much more so on the awesome days of Rosh Hashanah and Yom Kippur, days of renewal, of introspection and supplication for forgiveness, decisive days when everything we will encounter and experience in the coming year is prescribed!

These are indeed solemn days, but they are nevertheless festivals, days when we should have *simchah* (joy), confident in the knowledge that our loving Father in Heaven will bless us with all that is good. After chastising the people on Rosh Hashanah for their waywardness, the prophet Nehemiah said, "Do not be sad and do not weep …. Eat rich foods and drink sweet beverages, and send portions to those who have nothing prepared, for today is sacred to our Lord. Do not be sad; the enjoyment of Hashem is your strength" (*Nehemiah* 8:9-10).

In this spirit of solemnity and joy, let us look at the *tefillos* (prayers) of Rosh Hashanah and Yom Kippur, and see how they can help us bond with Hashem.

Happy Birthday, Humanity!

*R*osh Hashanah does not commemorate the day the world was created. Rather, it represents the *sixth* day of Creation, the day on which Hashem said, "Let us make man …" (*Genesis* 1:26).

Nowhere else in the account of Creation do we find Hashem saying, "Let *us*." Whose participation was Hashem seeking — and why only in the creation of man?

The Baal Shem Tov explains that all other living things were created in a state of completion. Animals are not required to voluntarily exert themselves to change. Caterpillars become butterflies because this transformation is programmed in their genes. The only creature that must make a voluntary effort to become something other than it was at creation is *man*. Job said that man comes into the world as "a wild mule" (*Job* 11:12), and man, by his own efforts, must change himself from an animal state into a spiritual human being. Had Hashem created man already spiritual, man would be an angel rather than a human being. Angels are *created* as spiritual beings, whereas man must *transform* himself into a spiritual individual. Hence, Hashem required man's participation in his own creation, and therefore He said, "Let *us* make man." We are indeed partners with Hashem in our creation as spiritual beings.

> *A tzaddik learned of a man whose berachos (blessings) appeared to be miraculously effective. He met this person, who was rather simple and unlearned. Initially the tzaddik thought that the man must be one of the "hidden tzaddikim," but as he observed him, he concluded that this was not so. The tzaddik then asked, "By what merit are your berachos always fulfilled?"*
>
> *The man responded, "The Baal Shem Tov said that we are partners with Hashem in our creation. I heard the rabbi of our shul say that if one partner makes a commitment, the other partner is obligated to honor it. So, when I give someone a berachah [blessing], I say,*

'Hashem, don't forget — we are partners. I promised
this person something, so please be sure to fulfill it.' "

That is the beauty of sincere, simple faith.

So, because Rosh Hashanah is our birthday, it is only fitting that we reflect on how well we are doing in exercising our share of the partnership.

Hashem gave each of us a *neshamah* (soul) with the potential for us to develop it.

> *A man invested $1,000 with a businessman. After*
> *a year, he asked how his investment was doing. The*
> *businessman returned the envelope containing the*
> *$1,000. The investor became very angry. "I gave you the*
> *money to invest for profit, not to lie idly in your desk!"*
>
> *The businessman said, "Let me have the money for*
> *another year. I'll see to it that it accrues profit."*
>
> *If at the end of the second year he returns the money*
> *with no growth, he is unlikely to be entrusted with it*
> *again.*
>
> *We ask Hashem for another year of life. If in the past*
> *year we have not improved the neshamah that He gave*
> *us, we must be certain to make an effort to improve it*
> *in the coming year.*

Nowadays there is a wondrous proliferation of books for the Jewish consumer, all written in a language that is readily understood. We have access to inspiring books of *mussar* (studies of self-discipline) and accounts of the lives of *tzaddikim* that can guide us toward developing our potential and encouraging our spiritual growth.

By making use of our intellect we can discover any number of ways to improve ourselves and make us worthy of being included as partners with Hashem.

L'Shanah Tovah Tikaseivu vs. Happy New Year

How different Rosh Hashanah is from the secular New Year! We assemble in shul, and, in a solemn albeit festive manner, pray to Hashem, our King, for another year of life and good fortune. In contradistinction, on December 31, many people celebrate the end of the year by becoming intoxicated, and at midnight they exclaim, "Happy New Year!"

For many people, one day is like another, and in pursuing their frenetic lifestyle, they rarely pause to reflect on what their lives are all about, and on what are their goals and ultimate purpose. As the new year approaches and the calendar changes, they are aroused to think, *What! Another year of my life is irretrievably gone! What do I have to show for it? Am I happier than I was a year ago? Hardly. Am I better off financially than I was a year ago? Not really. In fact, I may be more deeply in debt. Do I have reason to expect that in the new year I will be more successful? No.* These are depressing thoughts. One cannot declare "Happy New Year!" when one is depressed. Therefore, they drink to intoxication to forget their depression. Only then can they say, "Happy New Year!" On the following morning, they may awaken with a pounding headache, with no recollection of the "glorious happiness" of the previous night.

In contrast, Rosh Hashanah is preceded by the month of Elul, a month of introspection and soul-searching. We recognize the errors we may have made and we pray for forgiveness. At candle-lighting time or during *Kiddush,* we thank Hashem for sustaining us throughout the past year.

We then go to shul and find that the Rosh Hashanah *tefillah* is spiritually uplifting. We look forward to Hashem's blessing for the coming year. In this atmosphere, we turn to each other and say, "*L'Shanah tovah tikaseivu* — May Hashem inscribe you for a good year." Having utilized our time in shul wisely, we joyously go home for a festive Yom Tov meal with the family, and the following morning, we return to shul for solemn *tefillah.*

Yes, there is indeed a marked difference between Rosh Hashanah and New Year's Day.

Rosh Hashanah and Yom Kippur

Why did Hashem not arrange that Yom Kippur precede Rosh Hashanah? After having one's sins forgiven, a person would be in a much better position to be inscribed for a year of life, health, and happiness.

R' Yisrael Salant said that most people are preoccupied with their mundane wants and needs, and they would not have attained the necessary level to achieve the spiritual heights of Yom Kippur. Therefore, on Rosh Hashanah Hashem first ensures that they understand that they are being judged for their earthly deeds; that knowledge should inspire them to reflect on their actions of the past year and motivate them to *teshuvah*. On Yom Kippur they can then earn His forgiveness for having sinned.

Teshuvah is a unique Divine gift. The Talmud says that *teshuvah* was created before the universe (*Nedarim* 39b). Why? Because *teshuvah* is *l'ma'aleh min hateva*, beyond reality. It does not follow the rules of logic and reality, and therefore to bring *teshuvah* into a created world would mean defying the laws of reality, which is not how Hashem runs the world.

In reality, there can indeed be forgiveness for a crime, but the act cannot be undone. *Teshuvah* is unique. With sincere *teshuvah,* Hashem undoes the past and erases the act. It is as if the transgression never occurred!

The Midrash says, "They asked Wisdom, 'What is the sinner's punishment?' Wisdom answered, 'Sinners — let them be pursued by their evil.' They asked Prophecy, 'What is the sinner's punishment?' Prophecy answered, 'The soul that sins — it shall die.' They asked Torah, 'What is the sinner's punishment?' Torah answered, 'Let him bring a guilt-offering and gain atonement.' They asked Hashem, 'What is the sinner's punishment?' Hashem said, 'Let him do *teshuvah* and he will be forgiven.'" (*Pesikta D'Rav Kahana* 24:7). Only Hashem can provide the seemingly impossible "magic" of *teshuvah*.

There is indeed logic to *teshuvah*. Rambam says that *teshuvah* is more than just regretting one's sinful act. For *teshuvah* to be effective a decisive personality overhaul is required, so that this person is not the same person who committed the sin. It is only logical that Person B should not be punished for a sin committed by Person A. That may explain why the punishment, as exercised by humans, can be rescinded, but that does not undo the act. Only Hashem can accomplish that: "I will have wiped away your willful sins like a thick mist and your transgressions like a cloud" (*Isaiah* 44:22). When a mist has cleared, not a trace of it remains.

You know how exciting it is to trade in your old automobile, with its dented fenders and sluggish engine, for a spanking-new model. That is the impact of doing *teshuvah*. It can turn *you* into a brand-new model as well.

But merely reading the *Selichos* (prayers for forgiveness) is not enough. That brings to mind the doctor who prescribed medication but the patient failed to recover. The patient complained, "I read the prescription three times a day, just as you said." The doctor replied, "You fool! You were to have the prescription filled and to have taken the medication three times a day!" The *Selichos* are a prescription. Just reading them is not enough; we must follow through with action.

Teshuvah demands doing a thorough soul-searching, discovering the character defects that are innate in every human being — vanity, greed, envy, selfishness, lust — and transforming them into desirable traits. When we do our part, Hashem performs the miracle of creating us anew.

Beginning on Rosh Hashanah and throughout the Ten Days of Repentance, we do the soul-searching. On Yom Kippur we can achieve the spirituality of the heavenly angels and we are blessed with forgiveness. We then joyously participate in the festival of Succos, the season of our gladness.

Decreed on Rosh Hashanah

*O*n Rosh Hashanah, each individual's livelihood for the coming year is decided. A person would be very wise to spend as much time as he is able on Torah study and *tefillah*. Hashem will certainly take note and not penalize him or deduct from his preordained amount; rather, his actions will earn him reward.

> *The Maggid of Dubnow related a parable. A poor man came to a town where two wealthy men lived. One was a tightwad who never gave a cent for tzedakah (charity), while the other was a lavish benefactor who gave generously to tzedakah and his door was always open to the hungry poor.*
>
> *The poor man happened to knock on the door of the tightwad to ask for food. The tightwad said, "First, you must chop all the firewood in my yard." After working several hours, the needy man asked for food. The miser pointed to the house of the benefactor and said, "Go to that house and you will be fed." The pauper did as he was told and enjoyed a good meal.*

> *The poor man later told someone, "I worked hard for several hours, but it was worth it to get a good meal."*
> *When he related his day's activities, he was told, "You were exploited! The meal you ate you would have been given without doing any work at all!"*

So it is with us. We will be the beneficiaries of what is pre-ordained for us without becoming a workaholic and disregarding family, friends, obligations, etc. in a frenzied quest to earn more.

The High Holy Days Melodies

*M*any of the traditional chants of the High Holy Days services are universal. The very same melodies may be heard in Israel, Europe, America, South Africa, Australia: indeed, throughout the world.

Melodies are rich in associations, and can transport us back through time. They can also be more powerful than words.

> *In Chassidic lore, Leib Sarah's (Leib, the son of Sarah) is one of the most colorful personalities. R' Leib was a disciple of both the Baal Shem Tov and his successor, the Maggid of Mezeritch.*
> *In that era, Jews were not permitted to dwell in large*

cities, and the means by which they were allowed to earn a livelihood were limited. Some managed wayside inns in rural areas. Since they did not dwell in a town, their children had no access to a cheder (Hebrew school), and often the proprietor of an inn would engage a melamed (tutor) who would spend months at the inn teaching the innkeeper's children. R' Yosef, an elderly widower, was such a melamed.

One day, the local poritz (feudal lord) came to the inn, and when he saw the proprietor's beautiful daughter, he said, "I am taking that girl for a wife. I will come back tomorrow with a priest to conduct the ceremony."

Everyone was horrified. The powers of the poritz were absolute. He could imprison people at his whim. The daughter, Sarah, said, "I'll never let that fiend near me. I'll marry R' Yosef tonight. The priest will not allow the poritz to take a married woman."

R' Yosef said, "Child, what are you saying? I am an old man and you are but a child."

Sarah said, "There is no one else here whom I can marry before tomorrow. I must marry you, R' Yosef."

They were able to gather ten men for a minyan and Sarah married R' Yosef. She subsequently bore him a child,, whom they named Aryeh Leib.

R' Yosef did not live to see Aryeh Leib become a bar mitzvah. Before R' Yosef died, he told his son, "You were born due to your mother's mesiras nefesh [self-sacrifice] for Yiddishkeit. You must always be known by her name." Henceforth Aryeh Leib was known as R' Leib Sarah's.

R' Leib's mission was to rescue and ransom Jews from the dungeons of the poritzim, and he traveled far and wide. One Yom Kippur he found himself in a village where they were unable to form a minyan (quorum of at least ten adult males). One villager had left to spend Yom Kippur elsewhere, and thus there were only nine adult men, including R' Leib. R' Leib said, "I have never davened without a minyan on Yom Kippur. Isn't there a Jew anywhere nearby?" The congregants said there were no other Jewish men in the area.

Then someone spoke up. "There is one Jew, but he is no longer a Jew. He is the local poritz. When he was a young lad, he worked for the poritz, and the poritz's only child, a daughter, became enamored of him. The poritz told him that if he converted to Christianity, he could marry the daughter and eventually inherit the entire fiefdom. The lad, who had no family, converted, and he is now the poritz. He is a devout Christian and will have nothing to do with Jews."

R' Leib said, "A Jew is always a Jew. I will go to him."

The people tried to dissuade him. "He will turn his dogs on you."

But R' Leib was adamant. He went to the castle, and miraculously, the ferocious dogs ignored him. He confronted the poritz, who was taken aback by R' Leib's angelic appearance.

R' Leib said, "I am known as Leib, the son of Sarah," and told the poritz the origin of that appellation. "My mother sacrificed her life for her Jewishness, and you threw away your heritage. But it is never too late. There is always teshuvah. Tonight is Yom Kippur, and you can begin your teshuvah by completing the minyan."

Imagine the villagers' shock when they saw R' Leib return unharmed, accompanied by the poritz. When R' Leib began to chant the traditional Kol Nidrei, the poritz's eyes welled with tears as he heard the conventional melodies and recalled the Yom Kippurs of his youth. He joined in the prayers, and when everyone had finished, he continued to stand upright, praying tearfully. He remained on his feet all night and throughout the services the following day. At the close of Ne'ilah, he declared loudly, "Shema Yisrael!" and recited seven times, "Hashem, He is the God," then fell lifeless to the floor.

R' Leib told the villagers the Talmudic account of Elazar ben Doradia, a profligate sinner who died while weeping in repentance. A heavenly voice declared, "Elazar ben Doradia shall enter Gan Eden [Paradise]." R' Leib said, "The poritz, too, has done true teshuvah, and will merit Gan Eden."

The traditional melodies of Rosh Hashanah and Yom Kippur not only span decades of our lives, but also bind us to Jews throughout the world.

Minchah of Erev Rosh Hashanah

*W*hat is unique about the Minchah (afternoon prayer service) of Erev Rosh Hashanah? It is a standard weekday Minchah without any additions. True, but you were not privileged to hear my father, *zt"l, daven* this Minchah.

The Talmud states that "One day of a year can be considered an entire year" (*Rosh Hashanah* 2b). The Talmud also states, "Part of the day is like an entire day" (*Pesachim* 4a). Merge these two statements and we learn that part of a day = an entire day = an entire year.

These last few moments of the past year can encompass the entire year. This Minchah, which includes the last *Amidah* of the year, can be equivalent to all the *Amidahs* of the past year. When we *daven* this Minchah with proper *kavannah,* we can redeem any *Amidahs* we may have recited without the proper *kavannah.*

My father served as *chazzan* for this last Minchah of the year, and listening to his prayers was heartrending. Anyone who had not adequately prepared himself to do *teshuvah* during Elul was inspired to do so when they heard his *tefillah.*

After Minchah I heard several of the worshipers say, "We are certain to have a good year. The Rebbe attained it for us with his *davening*."

Let us *daven* this last *Amidah* of the year with the awareness of its far-reaching effects.

Heartfelt Prayers

*B*efore Rosh Hashanah, the Tzaddik of Sanz would relate this parable.

A prince once lost favor in his father's eyes and was exiled to a distant part of the empire. Never having had to work, he had no skills with which to support himself, so he hired himself out as a shepherd.

With the sun blazing overhead, he experienced extreme discomfort. He saw that other shepherds had constructed small huts to provide them with shade, but try as he might, he could not build a hut. Every attempt he made resulted in disaster.

After some time under these conditions, he heard that there was going to be a parade in honor of the king's visit, and the populace lined the roadside to watch the parade. There was a custom that a subject could write a request on a slip of paper and throw it toward the royal coach. Those petitions that fell into the coach would be granted.

The prince wrote a request for a hut to protect him

from the sun. At the parade, he threw the slip toward the coach and it landed inside. When the king read it, he recognized his son's handwriting and began to sob. "How terribly low my son has fallen," he said. "He could have requested to be forgiven and brought back to the palace, where he would lack for nothing. Yet, he now has no greater aspiration than to be granted a shepherd's hut!"

The Tzaddik wept. "We have the opportunity on Rosh Hashanah to petition the King. We could ask for the Redemption, to be taken back to Jerusalem with restoration of the Temple. Yet, all we ask for is our petty personal desires."

Before we pray, let us contemplate what it is that truly warrants our heartfelt prayers. Hashem is a benevolent Father and King, and our requests — worthwhile or trivial — will surely be heard.

Borchu

☞ *To Bless Hashem?*

*W*ith the very first words of Maariv, we encounter a challenge. "Bless Hashem, the Blessed One." *We* should bless Hashem? That sounds decidedly illogical. Also, what is meant by "the Blessed One"?

Some commentators explain that the word *berachah* is related to the word *bereichah*, which connotes a "spring." Hashem is referred to as a "Spring" from Whom all blessings flow (*Rashba, Teshuvos* 5:31). But that does not explain the Talmudic passage relating that the High Priest, R' Yishmael, entered the Holy of Holies on Yom Kippur, whereupon Hashem said to him, "Yishmael, My child, bless Me." R' Yishmael replied, "May it be Your will that Your mercy overwhelm Your anger, that Your mercy overcome Your Attributes, that You treat Your children with the Attribute of Mercy, and that for their sake You go beyond the boundary of judgment" (*Berachos* 7a). How are we to understand this?

Bnei Yisaschar cites the verse, "A king establishes his land with justice" (*Proverbs* 29:4), and states that Hashem conducts Himself totally within the framework of justice. Hashem's love is boundless, and He desires to bestow His kindness upon His children. "Even more than the calf wishes to suck, the cow wishes to suckle" (*Pesachim* 112a). Despite this, when Jews do not deserve His kindness, according to absolute justice, they are not worthy of Hashem's bestowing mercy on them.

Nonetheless, Hashem has given *tzaddikim* the power to overrule His decrees (*Moed Katan* 16b). The Talmud cites a case in which R' Eliezer differed with the Sages who were in the majority. A voice from heaven declared, "The halachah accords with R' Eliezer." The Sages disputed the voice, saying, "Hashem gave us the Torah, and the Torah states that the majority opinion rules" (*Bava Metzia* 59b). The Talmud tells us that the prophet Elijah revealed himself to the Sages and told them that Hashem was pleased because, "My children have triumphed over Me." That is, Hashem was pleased that the Sages ruled according to the dictates of the Talmud, and they did not allow the dictum to be waived by virtue of the heavenly voice.

The bounds of strict judgment should prevent Hashem from showing kindness to His children when they do not deserve it. But R' Yishmael had the power of a *tzaddik* to override Hashem's withholding His mercy; thus, Hashem bestowed His kindness on His undeserving children — and Hashem welcomed R' Yishmael's blessing.

You may ask, "That applies to a *tzaddik* like R' Yishmael, but how do *we* bless Hashem?" We do so by observing the Torah, which enables us to deserve His bounty so that He will exercise His mercy and show His kindness to us. This also explains the Midrash that states, "When Jews do the will of Hashem, they add power to His might" (*Eichah Rabbah* 1:35). How can anything be added to Hashem's infinite might? When we do the will of Hashem, we remove the hindrance to His kindness, thereby increasing, as it were, His ability to exercise His power.

The First Mitzvah

Until the *Amidah,* the Maariv service of Rosh Hashanah is the same as the Maariv of Shabbos and the festivals. However, there is one unique feature in this Maariv service.

It is a mitzvah to recite the *Shema* morning and evening. The *Shema* of the Rosh Hashanah Maariv is *the first mitzvah of the new year!*

The Talmud begins with the Mishnah, "From when on do we recite the *Shema* in the evening?" (*Berachos* 2a). The reason the Talmud opens with this theme is because a youth becomes a bar mitzvah at the onset of his 13th year; i.e., at the sundown of the last day of his 12th year. He is now an adult, obligated to perform all of the mitzvos of the Torah. His first mitzvah as an adult is reciting the *Shema*. For us the Maariv *Shema* is likewise our first mitzvah of the new year.

> *R' Zushe of Anipole concealed his identity by assuming the persona of an unlearned man, and asked R' Shmelke of Nikolsburg, an outstanding Torah scholar, to teach him Talmud.*
>
> *R' Shmelke began with the Mishnah in Berachos, "Me'eimasai korin es Shema be'arvis" and translated it as "From when do we recite the Shema in the evening?"*
>
> *R' Zushe began to tremble. "Why do you say that 'me'eimasai' means 'from when'?" he asked. "The word 'eimah' means 'dread,' and 'Me'eimasai korin es Shema be'arvis' means, 'Trembling with awe, one should recite the Shema.'"*
>
> *R' Shmelke said, "I don't have anything to teach you!"*

The *Shema* is our declaration of belief in the unity of Hashem and our acceptance of *ol malchus Shamayim* — the yoke of the heavenly kingdom. As the first mitzvah of the new year, it should set the tone for the upcoming year, stressing our awareness of the infinite majesty of Hashem and our total subjugation to His will.

Geulah D'Tefillah
Redemption and Prayer

*I*n many congregations, before beginning the *Amidah*, the practice is to recite the verses, "Blow the shofar at the moon's renewal, at the time appointed for our festive day. Because it is a decree for Israel, a judgment [day] for the God of Jacob" (*Psalms* 81:4-5).

There are authorities (the Gaon of Vilna, R' Shneur Zalman, author of *Tanya*) who disapprove of this practice. The paragraphs preceding the morning and evening *Amidah* speak of the Redemption from Egypt, and end with the *berachah*, "Blessed is Hashem, Who redeemed Israel." The Talmud says that the *Amidah* should follow immediately after the *berachah* of the Redemption (*Berachos* 4b), without any interruption. In Maariv we do add a paragraph, *Hashkiveinu*, which the Talmud considers an extension of the *berachah* of Redemption, because it states that Hashem saves us from many dangers. However, these authorities say that inserting verses from Scripture before the *Amidah* is not appropriate.

As noted above, *tefillah* is man approaching Hashem and communicating with Him. The Redemption from Egypt signifies Hashem coming close to His children, demonstrating His love for them, as Moses said, "Or has any god ever miraculously come to take for himself a nation from amidst a nation, with challenges, with signs, and with wonders … such as everything that Hashem, your God, did for you in Egypt before your eyes?" (*Deuteronomy* 4:34). Israel and Hashem thus approach each other through Redemption and *tefillah*, and this is why the two are juxtaposed (*Rav Schwab on Prayer*, pp. 401-405).

The justification for inserting the above phrase, "Sound the shofar, etc." may be because the Ultimate Redemption will be heralded by the sounding of a shofar, as is written, "It shall be on that day that a great shofar will be blown, and those who are lost in the land of Assyria and those cast away in the land of Egypt will come [together], and they will prostrate themselves to Hashem on the holy mountain in Jerusalem" (*Isaiah* 27:13). The verse is, therefore, germane to the concept of Redemption and is not considered an interruption between Redemption and *tefillah*.

Kaddish For The High Holy Days

Throughout the year, the text of the *Kaddish* reads, "Blessed, praised, glorified, exalted, extolled, mighty, upraised, honored, and lauded be the Name of the Holy One, Blessed is He, beyond any blessing and song, praise and consolation that are uttered in the world." From Rosh Hashanah through Yom Kippur we add one word, so that the text reads, "... Blessed is He, *exceedingly* beyond [lit., beyond and beyond] all blessings ...."

Levush (582:5) states that the reason for this addition is because during these days, "Hashem ascends from the Throne of Mercy and sits on the Throne of Judgment." This is a kabbalistic concept.

There may also be another explanation. The Talmud relates that R' Chanina overheard someone praising Hashem lavishly, using many superlative adjectives. When he had finished, R' Chanina said, "Well, have you exhausted all the praises due Hashem? If it were not that Moses said in the Torah, 'the great, mighty, and awesome God,' and the men of the Great Assembly incorporated these praises into the *tefillah*, we would not be permitted to say them" (*Berachos* 33b). In other words, listing a number of adjectives about Hashem limits the praise of Him, implying that these are His only praiseworthy Attributes. We may relate the various wonders Hashem has performed, but we do not add descriptive adjectives beyond those listed by Moses.

If we do add detailed depictions, we must provide a caveat stating that we realize what we are saying is not all-encompassing. Thus, following the Hymn of Glory, we recite the verse, "Who can express the mighty acts of Hashem, [who] can make all of His praise heard?" (*Psalms* 106:2), thereby declaring that we know that the praises have said are not exhaustive, because praise of Him is infinite.

On Rosh Hashanah and Yom Kippur, we do add many praises of Hashem. Therefore, to emphasize that we know these are not all-inclusive, in the *Kaddish* we add that Hashem is "*exceedingly* beyond all blessing and song, praise, and consolation that are uttered in the world."

☞ *Remember Us for Life*

זָכְרֵנוּ לְחַיִּים
Remember us for life ....

Upon completing the first *berachah* of the *Amidah*, we add, "Remember us for life, O King Who desires life, and inscribe us in the Book of Life — for Your sake, O Living God."

This follows the words of the first *berachah*, "Who recalls the kindnesses of the Patriarchs." We ask that just as Hashem remembers the many virtues of our ancestors, He should remember us to extend His kindness to us, their descendants.

What is meant by the phrase, "for Your sake, O Living God?"

When Moses pleaded to be allowed to enter the Holy Land, Rashi says that although he could have invoked the merits of his good deeds, he simply asked for Divine grace, because that is what *tzaddikim* do (*Deuteronomy* 3:23). The commentaries add, "But *tzaddikim* never invoke their merits, because they always feel that they have fallen short of fulfilling Hashem's will." The answer is that *tzaddikim* indeed do not ask anything of Hashem by virtue of the good deeds that they *have done* in the past. Rather, they invoke the merits of the good deeds *that they will do* in the future.

So it is with us. We say in the morning service, "What gain is there in my death, in my descent to the pit? Will the dust acknowledge You? Will it declare Your truth?" (*Psalms* 30:10). We pray for life by virtue of the praises of Hashem that we will offer if we live. Hence we say, "Remember us for life… for Your sake, O Living God," i.e., so that we may continue to praise You,

R' Levi Yitzchak from Berditchev has a charming explanation for why we request, "Inscribe us in the Book of Life." He says that if a person tells a friend that he wishes to give him a gift, the friend trusts that he will indeed do so. However, if the friend knows that there are those who may try to dissuade the benefactor from giving him the gift, he may say, "Thank you, but please put in writing that you will do so, so that my enemies, seeing that I have a guarantee, will not try to dissuade you."

We know that Hashem wishes to grant us life. However, we may have committed sins that created accusatory angels (*Ethics of the Fathers* 4:13). These angels may argue that we do not deserve Hashem's beneficence. We, therefore, say, "Please, Hashem, inscribe us for life. Make it a matter of record that You are granting us life. In that way, accusatory angels will not try to convince You to do otherwise."

It is noteworthy that at this point we pray, "Remember us for life," but we do not say, "for a good life." At the end of the *Amidah* we say, "And inscribe all the children of Your covenant for a good life." Why the difference?

What is a good life? King David states, "As for me, closeness to Hashem is my good" (*Psalms* 73:28). *Mesillas Yesharim* (Chapter 1) comments, "Being close to Hashem is the only true good. Whatever else people consider to be good is illusory."

At the beginning of the *Amidah*, we ask Hashem for the gift of life, which is solely a gift from Him. However, for it to be a "good life" requires our participation. During the *Amidah* we prayed for Hashem to reveal Himself to all mankind, and in the prayer of *Modim* we acknowledge Hashem's kindnesses and express our gratitude to Him. We have thus taken several steps to bring us closer to Hashem. Therefore, we may now ask for a "good life."

The Maggid of Kamenitz says that "Remember us for life, for Your sake, O Living God" means that we are asking Hashem to grant us life so that we can do His will. The Maggid illustrates with a parable.

> *A young man who was drafted by the army appealed for an exemption because he had an elderly mother whom he was responsible to support. The draft board sent an investigator, who found the old woman living in a wretched hut.*
>
> *"Does your son support you?" he asked.*

> *The old woman said, "My son? I haven't seen him in several years. He will have nothing to do with me. I survive through the charity of others."*
>
> *Obviously, this son will not receive an exemption from the draft.*

We ask Hashem to grant us life so that we can do His will. But if we spend most of our time satisfying our own desires rather than doing Hashem's will, can we have the audacity to ask to be granted life?

It is always imperative to pray for life.

Why was the prayer to be remembered for life inserted in the first *berachah* of the *Amidah*, the *berachah* of the Patriarchs?

The Talmud states that *tzaddikim* are referred to as living even after their physical death, and *resha'im* (wicked people) are referred to as dead even when they are physically alive (*Berachos* 18a-b). Although both human beings and animals have a physical existence, human life should be different than that of animals. Animals are driven solely by their physical urges and are totally self-centered. Animals have no concept of *chesed* (lovingkindness), of giving of oneself for the sake of others.

Spirituality consists of motivation and behavior beyond self-gratification, and animals in the wild are incapable of this. *Resha'im*, who are totally self-centered, are what science refers to as *homo sapiens*, animals with intellect. As a higher form of animal life they are indeed alive, but, since they are lacking spirituality, the human element within them is dead.

The patriarch Abraham, in rebelling against the self-gratifying pagan religions, promulgated *chesed* as the defining feature of humanity, and it is *chesed* that gives us the distinction of being alive as human beings rather than as intellectual animals.

When we pray for life, we pray for a dignified, truly human, spiritual life, a life of *chesed*. This is why this prayer is contained in the blessing, *Magen Avraham*. Hashem protects the nucleus of *chesed* bequeathed to us by Abraham.

> *When I was a child in Milwaukee, I was acquainted with an elderly man known as "der alte Shaya [the old Isaiah]." Shaya claimed he was 102, but others from his shtetl said he was actually 104.*
>
> *One Rosh Hashanah, Shaya was wearing his tallis, walking up and down the aisle with his finger in his machzor, but his lips were not moving. I asked him, "Reb Shaya, don't you daven?"*
>
> *Shaya wagged his finger at me and said, "After you have davened for 96 years, you can stop, too."*
>
> *Very cute — but very wrong. One should always pray for life, even at the age of 104.*

☙ *A Plea for Earthly Life*

מִי כָמוֹךָ אַב הָרַחֲמִים, זוֹכֵר יְצוּרָיו לְחַיִּים בְּרַחֲמִים.

Who is like You, Merciful Father,
Who recalls His creatures mercifully for life!

This verse is inserted after the paragraph in which we say, "Who is like You, O Master of mighty deeds, and who is comparable to You, O King Who causes death and restores life …," and before the verse that reads, "You are faithful to revivify the dead."

We believe that there is an afterlife, and that the *neshamah* will continue to exist after we leave this world. Yet, we very much desire life in this earthly world.

The *sefarim* tell us that prior to our creation, our *neshamos* existed in a supernal world. When Hashem created man, the Torah says "*vayitzer adam* — He formed man" (*Genesis* 2:7) and the word וַיִּיצֶר, *vayitzer* (formed), is spelled with two *yuds*. Rashi explains that this represents a twofold creation: one for this world and one for the world after the Revivification of the Dead.

In praying for earthly existence, we refer to *yotzer yetzurav lechaim* — the twofold creation. Life in the world of *neshamos* is indeed desirable, but we are asking Hashem for life in this, the earthly world.

☞ *We Are Indeed Grateful*

וּבְכֵן תֵּן פַּחְדְּךָ ה׳ אֱלֹקֵינוּ עַל כָּל מַעֲשֶׂיךָ
And so, too, O Hashem, our God,
instill Your awe upon all Your works ....

In this paragraph we rectify a shortcoming of our ancestors.

When Hashem spoke to the Israelites during the Revelation at Sinai, they were so awestruck by the voice of Hashem that they asked Moses to intercede for them, because they feared they would not survive hearing the voice of Hashem (*Deuteronomy* 5:20-24). Hashem was pleased, and said, "Who can assure that this heart should always be theirs, to fear Me ..." (ibid. 5:26).

The Talmud relates that Moses chastised the Israelites, "Ingrates, descendants of an ingrate!" (*Avodah Zarah* 5b). Adam was an ingrate, because Hashem gave him Eve, the ideal wife, yet he blamed Eve for his sin, saying "The woman whom You gave to be with me — she gave me of the tree and I ate" (Rashi, *Genesis* 3:12).

In what way were the Israelites ingrates? Moses told them that when Hashem said, "Who can assure that this heart should always be theirs, to fear Me," they should have said, "*You* assure that we are instilled with this everlasting awe." Tosafos explain that the Israelites did not want to ask Hashem because they did not wish to be beholden to Him; this was their refusal to be grateful.

We right this wrong when we ask Hashem to give us — and all His creations — *yiras Shamayim,* reverence for and awe of the majesty of Hashem.

☞ Not a Self-Centered Request

וּבְכֵן תֵּן כָּבוֹד ה׳ לְעַמֶּךְ

And so, too, Hashem, grant honor to Your people

We do not seek personal glory. The psalmist makes this perfectly clear. "Not for our sake, Hashem, not for our sake, but for Your Name's sake give glory .... Why should the nations say, 'Where now is their God?' Our God is in the heavens; whatever He pleases, He does" (*Psalms* 115:1-3).

We know that we may not deserve Hashem's kindness, but if we are downtrodden, it is a *chillul Hashem* — an insult to Hashem, because the nations of the world will deny Hashem's Omnipotence and His selection of Israel as His chosen people.

This is a powerful prayer. When the Israelites committed the sin of the Golden Calf, Moses turned away the wrath of Hashem by saying, "Why should Egypt say the following: 'With evil intent did He take them out, to kill them in the mountains and to annihilate them from the face of the earth'?" (*Exodus* 32:12). And again, when the Israelites listened to the negative report of the Spies and Hashem wished to destroy them, Moses pleaded, "Then the nations that heard of Your fame will say, 'Because Hashem lacked the ability to bring this people to the Land that He had sworn to give them, He slaughtered them in the Wilderness'" (*Numbers* 14:15-16). "And Hashem said, 'I have forgiven because of your word'" (ibid. 14:20). The argument that evil occurring to Israel constitutes a *chillul Hashem* resulted in our being forgiven.

We ask Hashem to grant honor to His people because that will bring Him glory.

☞ The Joy of the Righteous

וּבְכֵן צַדִּיקִים יִרְאוּ וְיִשְׂמָחוּ

And so, too, the righteous will see and be glad ....

The question of why the righteous experience suffering is a vexing one. The Talmud says that Moses posed this question to Hashem, but Hashem told him that this concept is beyond the capacity of a human being to understand (*Berachos* 7a).

The psalmist says, "A boor cannot know, nor can a fool understand this: When the wicked bloom like grass and all the doers of iniquity blossom …" (*Psalms* 92:7-8). The verse continues, "… it is to destroy them till eternity." That is, the seeming good that the wicked experience is their reward on this world, but they will not have a portion in the World to Come.

We have absolute faith in the justice of Hashem, and it pains us when others deny it. When the Redemption occurs and Hashem will "remove evil's domination from the earth," as the prayer continues, the righteous, upright, and devout will rejoice in the manifestation of Hashem's justice, which will then be apparent to everyone.

☞ Recognition of Hashem's Exclusive Reign

וְתִמְלוֹךְ אַתָּה ה׳ לְבַדֶּךָ עַל כָּל מַעֲשֶׂיךָ
Then You, Hashem,
will reign alone over all Your works

These prayers refer to the time of the Redemption, when the entire world will acknowledge the sovereignty of Hashem.

We may think that this prediction does not apply to us, because we already believe in the sovereignty of Hashem. However, our belief may be lacking quality.

Moses warned the Israelites that when they achieve success and wealth, "And you may say in your heart, 'My strength and the might of my hand made me all this wealth" (*Deuteronomy* 8:17). Yes, we believe in Hashem, but we may nevertheless think that we, too, have a hand in our success. "Then you shall remember Hashem, your God, that it is He Who gives you strength to make wealth …" (ibid. 8:18).

It was due to Adam's sin that Hashem said, "By the sweat of your brow shall you eat bread …" (*Genesis* 3:19). We must do something to earn a livelihood, and indeed, the Torah says "Hashem will bless you in all your handiwork that you may undertake" (*Deuteronomy* 14:29). However, we are not to think that the amount of effort we expend determines the degree of our success or lack of success.

> *The Chofetz Chaim related a parable about a passenger on a train; the man was pushing against the foremost wall of the car. When asked what he was doing, he said, "I'm trying to make the train go faster."*
>
> *Obviously, his efforts are futile. His pushing on the wall has no effect whatsoever on the speed of the train.*
>
> *"Neither," said the Chofetz Chaim, "does your expenditure of effort increase your success."*

Yes, we believe that Hashem controls the world, but we think that we, too, contribute to the resulting outcome. The Torah perspective is that Hashem does not control our ethical and moral behavior, and we have free choice in these areas. But with the exception of these, Hashem controls everything.

With the Redemption, the fog that clouds our perception will be lifted, and we will realize that Hashem alone reigns over everything.

This theme is continued in the next paragraph. In the daily *Amidah* we say, "You are holy and Your Name is holy, and holy ones praise you every day, forever. Blessed are You, Hashem, the holy God." The latter appellation of Hashem, *Keil*, refers to the attribute of *chesed*, as it is written " *chesed Keil kol hayom* — the kindness of God is all day long (*Psalms* 52:3).

During the Days of Awe, Rosh Hashanah through Yom Kippur,

Hashem expects us to function at a more lofty level of spirituality, so that we can pass the test of *din* (judgment). Hence we say, "You are holy and Your Name is awesome, *and there is no power other than You,* as it is written, 'Hashem, Master of Legions, will be lofty in judgment and the holy God will be sanctified in righteousness.' Blessed are You, Hashem, the holy King."

The Simchah of Rosh Hashanah and Yom Kippur

☞ *Yom HaZikaron*

אַתָּה בְחַרְתָּנוּ מִכָּל הָעַמִּים אָהַבְתָּ אוֹתָנוּ וְרָצִיתָ בָּנוּ
You have chosen us from all the peoples.
You loved us and found favor in us.

As was noted above, although Rosh Hashanah and Yom Kippur are days of awe and solemnity, they are nevertheless festivals, and the prophet Nehemiah instructed the people not to be sad, but to rejoice.

What greater *simchah* can there be than a true realization of how fortunate we are that Hashem has chosen us to be His people.

In the daily morning service, we say, "We are fortunate — how good is our portion, how pleasant our lot, and how beautiful our heritage!" If I were the rabbi of a shul, I would have the worshipers join hands and dance with a fervor as intense as that of *Simchas Torah*. If we do not rejoice in being Hashem's children, we are indeed ingrates.

But this prayer may also be a request to Hashem to relieve our sufferings and distress in exile, and bring us back to our favored status. Many *tzaddikim*, most notably R' Levi Yitzchak of Berditchev, pleaded for the Redemption by virtue of Hashem's selecting us as His chosen people.

A woman came to the Maggid of Kozhnitz and complained that her husband was leaving her. "He says that he no longer loves me, and that I am not attractive."

The Maggid said, "What can I do, my poor woman, if he is so foolish to leave the marriage because he does not find you attractive? I cannot make a fool wise."

The woman wailed, "But Rabbi," she said, "many years ago, when we were married, I was very beautiful. Now that I have lost my beauty due to old age, is it fair that he should cast me away?"

The Maggid stood, and his eyes welled with tears. "Master of the universe," he said. "Listen to this woman. We, too, in our youth were beautiful to You. We followed You with perfect faith into the Wilderness, into an unsown desert. But now that we have lost that beauty, is it fair that You cast us away?"

Rosh Hashanah is indeed a *Yom HaZikaron*, a day of remembrance. Both Hashem and we ourselves should remember our beauty of yore. Unlike the elderly woman, who unfortunately cannot restore the beauty of her youth, we, *Klal Yisrael* (the Jewish people), can indeed do so. We can say this prayer with both joy and tears.

☞ Reaching Up to Hashem

יַעֲלֶה וְיָבֹא וְיַגִּיעַ וְיֵרָאֶה וְיֵרָצֶה וְיִשָּׁמַע וְיִפָּקֵד וְיִזָּכֵר ...
*May there rise, come, reach, be noted, be favored,
be heard, be considered, and be remembered ....*

The kabbalists say that Hashem desired to have a presence in this earthly world, and that is indeed how the world began. However, with each sin of mankind — sins committed by Adam, the generation of the Flood, the generation of the Tower of Babel, Sodom and Gomorrah, etc. — the Divine Spirit distanced itself further, ascending gradually through the eight levels of the supernal world. In this prayer, we ask that our prayers ascend to the highest level. Therefore, we use eight expressions of communication: rise, come, reach, etc.

As noted in the ArtScroll *Machzor*, Rabbi Samson Raphael Hirsch explains the eight expressions thus:

May our personal behavior and fortune *rise* above ordinary human existence; and *come* before Hashem to merit His interest; may nothing prevent them from *reaching* Hashem and gaining His acceptance; may they be *noted* in the best possible light; may they be worthy of Hashem's *favor*; may Hashem *hear* the impact these remembrances have on our lives; may Hashem *consider* our needs; and may He *remember* us and our relationship to Him.

☞ The Universal Recognition of Hashem

מְלוֹךְ עַל כָּל הָעוֹלָם כֻּלּוֹ בִּכְבוֹדֶךְ
Our God and God of our forefathers,
reign over the entire universe in Your glory

The prophet Isaiah predicts that after the Redemption, "The earth will be as filled with knowledge of Hashem as water covering the seabed" (*Isaiah* 11:9).

Although many people believe in God, their understanding of God is limited and superficial.

> *R' Shlomo Eiger, a noted Talmudist and a son of the great R' Akiva Eiger, was among those who did not look with favor at Chassidus. When his son, R' Leibele Eiger, joined the followers of the Rebbe of Kotzk, R' Shlomo was disappointed.*
>
> *When R' Leibele returned home after an extended period in Kotzk, his father asked him, "What did you learn in Kotzk?"*
>
> *R' Leibele responded, "I learned that Hashem is in full charge of the world.*
>
> *R' Shlomo summoned one of the kitchen maids. "Who is in charge of the world?" he asked.*
>
> *The woman responded, "Hashem, of course."*
>
> *R' Leibele pithily retorted, "She **says**. I **know**!"*

We pray for the time that the next verse in the prayer will be fulfilled: "Let everything that has been made know that You are its Maker, let everything that has been molded understand that You are its Molder...."

> *The Baal Shem Tov's grandson, R' Moshe Chaim Ephraim, related that the Baal Shem Tov once told of a fiddler who played a cheerful tune. It was so compelling that people began dancing. A deaf person came along, but because he could not hear the music, he thought that all those who were dancing had gone mad.*
>
> *We hear the music of Hashem and we dance to it. The rest of the world is deaf to the music and assumes that we are mad.*

This paragraph of the prayer concludes, "Blessed are You, Hashem ... Who sanctifies Israel and the Day of Remembrance." When Rosh Hashanah falls on a Shabbos, the closing words are, "Who sanctifies the Sabbath, Israel, and the Day of Remembrance."

Hashem sanctified the seventh day of each week to be Shabbos, and this consecration is not affected by variances in the calendar. The festivals, however, are determined by the calendar established by the Rabbinic Court, which sets the first day of the month according to the appearance of the new moon. Hence, it is Hashem's sanctification of Israel that has empowered its Sages to set the calendar and the days of the festivals, including the Day of Remembrance.

Psalm 24

לְדָוִד מִזְמוֹר לַה׳ הָאָרֶץ וּמְלוֹאָהּ ...
*Of David, a psalm. Hashem's is the
earth and its fullness ....*

In numerous congregations, Psalm 24 is recited after Maariv.
According to the kabbalah, this psalm is a *segulah* (spiritual rem-
edy) for *parnassah* (sustenance; livelihood).

Why is this psalm propitious for *parnassah*? The rebbe, R'
Shalom of Belz, cited verse 5, "He will receive a blessing from
Hashem, and just kindness from the God of his salvation."

As mentioned above, Moses cautioned the Israelites not to
think, "My strength and the might of my hand made me all this
wealth" (*Deuteronomy* 8:17). Rather, one should recognize that
his success is a blessing from Hashem. However, even if one may
indeed realize that his success is a blessing from Hashem, he may
also feel that he is righteous and has merited this blessing. Therefore, one should know that the blessing is a kindness from Hashem,
not one that has been earned.

מִי יַעֲלֶה בְהַר ה׳ וּמִי יָקוּם בִּמְקוֹם קָדְשׁוֹ
*Who can ascend the mountain of Hashem,
and who can stand in His holy place?*

We have spent the month of Elul doing *teshuvah*, identifying
our character defects and seeking to improve them. However, it
may happen that after Yom Kippur we regress to business as usual,
forfeiting the spirituality we have gained.

It is one thing to ascend a mountain, but if one is not careful, one may rapidly slip all the way down. It is not enough that we ascend the mountain of Hashem. We must continue to exert effort so that we remain standing at the lofty height we have achieved.

☞ *The Symbolic Foods*

It is traditional to eat certain foods during the *seudah* (festive meal) on the first night of Rosh Hashanah and to recite a brief prayer. I.e., we eat a slice of apple dipped in honey and ask for a "year that is good and sweet." We recognize that there are sometimes blessings in disguise, where the good may packaged in an unpleasant wrapper. Therefore, it is not enough to pray for a good year, but for a good, *sweet* year, in which we will experience the good as pleasant.

It is also traditional (from Rosh Hashanah until the end of Succos) to dip the challah on which we will recite the *hamotzi* blessing into honey. *Bnei Yisaschar* points out that the Hebrew word for honey (*devash*) has the same numerical value as *Av HaRachamim* (Merciful Father).

Other symbolic foods that we eat include the head of a fish (or of a lamb), while reciting the supplication, "May we be 'heads' [leaders] and not tails [followers]"; pomegranates, while reciting, "May we have abundant mitzvos, like the seeds of the pomegranate"; any food that connotes abundance, including a variety of beans known as *rubia*, Aramaic for "many," and carrots, which in Yiddish are *mehren*, translated as "to increase," and a variety of other foods that have a symbolic meaning.

Well and good, but why the symbolism? Why not just say the prayers?

The Talmud (*Berachos* 58a) states, "The kingdom of Heaven operates similarly to the earthly kingdom." There is a tribunal, with both accusatory and defending angels. There are angels that convey our prayers to Hashem, and there is Satan and his company, who seek to thwart our prayers from access to Hashem.

As wily as Satan is, he can be outsmarted. One of the purposes of sounding the shofar is to confuse Satan. Similarly, Satan may seek to block our prayers, but he does not have the ability to understand our gestures. Therefore, we resort to symbolic foods to represent our prayers.

When we recite the *Kiddush*, we say the *Shehechiyanu* blessing, thanking Hashem for sustaining us until this auspicious moment. This blessing is recited on special occasions, like the once-a-year festivals, or when one eats a new fruit or buys a new garment. Hence it is recited in conjunction with the Rosh Hashanah *Kiddush*.

On the second night of Rosh Hashanah, it is recommended that we serve a new fruit that we have not eaten the past year, which thus warrants the *Shehechiyanu* blessing. The Talmud explains that there is reason to consider the two days of Rosh Hashanah as one extended day. In that event, there would be no reason to say the *Shehechiyanu* blessing, since it was said previously on that day. Therefore, to satisfy all opinions, we eat a new fruit for which the *Shehechiyanu* blessing is authorized in its own right.

Shacharis

Master of the Universe

אֲדוֹן עוֹלָם ...
Master of the universe ....

Although *Adon Olam* is a prayer that is recited each and every day, it does possess a unique quality on Rosh Hashanah and Yom Kippur, because the *chazzan* for *Pesukei D'Zimrah* begins Shacharis by chanting *Adon Olam* using a melody that is reserved for the High Holy Days.

Rav Sherira Gaon said that if a person recites *Adon Olam* with proper *kavannah,* he can be assured that his prayers will be accepted and that no adversary will interfere with his prayers.

Inasmuch as the concept of "kingship" permeates the High Holy Days prayers, beginning the day with *Adon Olam* is most appropriate.

> *My father often told a story about a man who told the proprietor of a Judaica store that he wished to buy a siddur. When the proprietor showed him a siddur, he said, "No, I want a larger one." He rejected each of the*

*larger siddurim that he was shown, until the proprietor
showed him the Otzar HaTefillos, a massive siddur with
many pages of commentary.*

*Inasmuch as the customer did not appear to be
particularly scholarly, the proprietor asked why he would
want this massive siddur.*

*The customer explained, "I have small children,
and they like to play 'shul,' using my siddur. The first
few pages invariably become torn, so I lose the Adon
Olam. The Otzar HaTefillos siddur has many pages of
commentary at the beginning, so even if these pages are
torn out, I won't lose the Adon Olam!"*

My father told this story to point out the need for precaution-
ary measures to protect the mitzvos, so that even if they are played
with — i.e., tampered with — the essence of the mitzvah remains
intact. But the story also has a literal meaning. *Adon Olam* can be
regarded as the essence of *tefillah*.

The Gaon of Vilna came across a *sefer* stating that the reason we
begin Shacharis with *Adon Olam* is because the Midrash says that
the patriarch Abraham was the first person to refer to Hashem as
Adon (Lord, Master) (*Genesis* 15:8). We, therefore, use the term
Adon to invoke the merits of the patriarch in our behalf. The Gaon
had high praise for this insight.

Inherent in the realization of Hashem as Master is the understanding that we are his *avadim* (slaves). The word *eved*, "slave,"
generally has a negative connotation, but not in reference to our
relationship to Hashem. The greatest honor a person can attain is
to be called an *eved Hashem*.

A slave has no will of his own. He must do whatever his master commands. Similarly, a person should subjugate himself totally before Hashem, and "treat His will as if it were your will" (*Ethics of the Fathers* 2:4).

אֲשֶׁר מָלַךְ בְּטֶרֶם כָּל־יְצִיר נִבְרָא ... וְהוּא אֶחָד וְאֵין שֵׁנִי, לְהַמְשִׁיל לוֹ
Who reigned before any form was created ....
He is one — there is no second to compare to Him.

In our prayers, we find the verse, "Hashem reigns, Hashem has reigned, Hashem shall reign for all eternity." This verse is not found in Scripture; the Sages composed this text by juxtaposing segments of several verses to formulate the awe-inspiring phrasing. It is of note that the Sages depart from the usual sequence of *past, present, future*, and instead express Hashem's reign as *present, past, future*.

The reason is that in the present we see a universe in which many things exist, both in the macrocosm and microcosm. The Torah *hashkafah* (philosophy of life) is expressed in the prayer, "It was You before the world was created, it is You since the world was created." *Tanya* explains that Hashem is unchanging, unaffected by time, by place, or by any event in the universe.

We recognize that before Creation, Hashem alone existed, and He alone will exist when the world ceases to be. Therefore, we assert our belief that in the present, although we see many things that exist in the universe, the only true existence in the present is Hashem, just as He was in the past, prior to Creation, and as He will be in the future, after the world ceases to be.

The commentaries remark that when we say the verse, "It is

He Who was, He Who is, and He Who shall remain, in splendor," we should intend these words to be a declaration that whenever we mention Hashem's Name, we are asserting our belief in His eternity.

☞ The *Piyutim* (Liturgical Poems)

The *siddur* (prayer book) has undergone a complex development throughout Jewish history.

Tefillah has been a powerful force since Biblical times. There are numerous instances of people who prayed. King David said, "Evening, morning, and noon, I supplicate and moan; and He has heard my voice" (*Psalms* 55:18). Formal prayer appears to have been formulated by the Men of the Great Assembly, the body of Torah authority during the beginning of the Second Temple era (approx. 4th century BCE). They compiled the *Amidah* (*Shemoneh Esrei*) and numerous other prayers and *berachos*.

Several prayers in the *siddur* were composed by the Talmudic Sages. After the Talmudic era, we begin to find *piyutim* (liturgical poems), written by Torah scholars during the early and later Middle Ages. Some of these authors have been identified. Among the most prolific was R' Elazar HaKalir, who wrote several hundred *piyutim*. Many *piyutim* were composed specifically for various festivals, fast days, and other special occasions.

Piyutim have been inserted into the Rosh Hashanah and Yom Kippur *machzorim*, but the poetry was not universally accepted as part of the liturgy. The famous Torah commentator, Avraham ibn Ezra, was sharply critical of *piyutim* (see his commentary on *Ecclesiastes* 5:1).

The perspective regarding *piyutim* varies among congregations. Practically speaking, those *piyutim* that have been more widely accepted appear in the *machzor* in a large bold font. Some have been accorded special significance, in that the *Aron Kodesh* (Ark of the Torah) is opened when they are recited.

הַמֶּלֶךְ יוֹשֵׁב עַל כִּסֵּא רָם וְנִשָּׂא.
O King, Who is sitting upon a high and lofty throne.

In general, a different *chazzan* takes over for the main segment of Shacharis, which begins with the word *HaMelech* (the King). This is chanted in a loud voice, and the congregation responds, *"HaMelech."* (Please refer to the essay entitled "Kingship" p. 10.)

The verbal emphasis on the word *HaMelech* is meant to arouse the worshipers to be aware of the profound awesomeness of this day. The entire focus of the Rosh Hashanah *davening* is to acknowledge that Hashem is in charge of the world. And to recognize that on this day Hashem is sitting in judgment on the world and on every individual.

The paragraph that follows reads:

By the mouth of *yesharim* (the upright) shall You be exalted;
By the words of *tzaddikim* (the righteous) shall You be blessed;
By the tongue of *chassidim* (the devout) shall You be sanctified;
And amid *kedoshim* (the holy) shall You be lauded.

The prayer then continues, "And in the assemblies of the myriads of Your people ... shall Your Name be glorified, our King, throughout every generation."

> *One of the tzaddikim, about whom we know very little other than that his name was Menele and that he was R' Ahron of Karlin's uncle and a disciple of the Baal Shem Tov, used to say:*
>
> *It says, "By the mouth of yesharim shall You be exalted." It does not say, "By the mouth of Menele."*
>
> *It says, "By the words of tzaddikim shall You be blessed." It does not say, "By the words of Menele."*
>
> *It says, "By the tongue of chassidim shall You be sanctified." It does not say, "By the tongue of Menele."*
>
> *It says, "Amid kedoshim shall You be lauded." It does not say, "Amid Menele."*
>
> *Where, then, is Menele? Ah! "In the assemblies of the myriads of Your people ... shall Your Name be glorified." That is where Menele is found.*

This *tzaddik's* humility and self-effacement were profound. He did not feel that he, as an individual, was worthy of approaching Hashem; rather, he dared approach Hashem only as a member of the assembly of *Klal Yisrael*.

Approaching Hashem as an individual may be more terrifying than one can bear, but if one is part of a *tzibbur* (community), the fear is mitigated.

The Talmud gives great importance to *tefillah b'tzibbur* (communal prayer). One commentary states that one hundred people who pray in the same room do not necessarily constitute a *tzibbur*. If each person prays for his own needs, then the group is made up of one hundred *individuals*, and is not a genuine *tzibbur*. When each individual prays for all the others as well as for himself, that unquestionably constitutes *tefillah b'tzibbur*.

When we join with others in true brotherhood, then we can say, "… with joyous song shall Your Name be glorified."

With what is known today about "multisensory perception," there is no need to ascribe anything supernatural to the following incident.

> *A chassid of R' Mordechai of Lechovitch never missed experiencing Rosh Hashanah with his rebbe. One year, he was in Leipzig on business, and could not make it back in time. He went to a local shul, but was heartbroken because he was not with the rebbe. Suddenly, he heard the rebbe's voice crying out, "HaMelech!" His heart jumped for joy.*
>
> *On his next visit to Lechovitch, he heard the rebbe comment on the verse in the Megillah, "Venishma pisgam hamelech asher yaaseh bechal malchuso — The king's decree which he will proclaim shall be heard throughout all his kingdom …" (Esther 1:20). The rebbe asserted, "When someone declares, 'HaMelech!' it can be heard even as far as Leipzig."*

☞ *Psalm 130*

שִׁיר הַמַּעֲלוֹת
A Song of Ascents

(In some congregations, this psalm is chanted by the *chazzan* with responsive reading by the congregation. The *Aron Kodesh* may be opened.)

This is one of fifteen Songs of Ascents, corresponding to the fifteen steps whereby one ascended to the Sanctuary in the Temple. Even though today we do not have the Temple, when reading this psalm one should feel as if he is approaching the innermost chambers of holiness.

מִמַּעֲמַקִּים קְרָאתִיךָ ה׳
From the depths I called You, Hashem.

The term *mima'amakim* is used, rather than the term *me'omek*. The latter means "depths," whereas *mima'amakim* means "many depths." Even when a person feels totally crushed by many problems, he should not despair but call out to Hashem.

R' Nachman of Breslov describes his moments of profound depression and says, "Even in the depths of depression, I did not lose hope. I recalled the verse, 'If I ascend to heaven, You are there; if I make my bed in the lowest depths, behold! You are there ...' (*Psalms* 139:8). Even if I was in the lowest of depths, I was not alone, because Hashem is everywhere, and He was with me there."

ה׳ שִׁמְעָה בְקוֹלִי
Hashem, hear my voice.

Even if I do not know the proper words with which to pray to You, listen to the supplicating tone of my voice.

— 74 —

כִּי עִמְּךָ הַסְּלִיחָה לְמַעַן תִּוָּרֵא
For with You is forgiveness, that You may be feared.

In what way does Hashem's forgiveness lead us to fear of Him? Because if there were no forgiveness, a sinful person might think, *What is the use of changing my ways? I am beyond redemption.* Therefore, the psalmist says, "Never despair of coming close to Hashem. He will forgive your sins, and you can lead a life of *yiras Shamayim* — fear and awe of Hashem.

קִוִּיתִי ה׳ קִוְּתָה נַפְשִׁי
My soul yearns for Hashem.

R' Hillel of Paritsch once noticed a man weeping during davening. When R' Hillel inquired why he was weeping, the man said, "I am crying out of pity for my neshamah. It was in heaven in a totally spiritual world, now it has come down to be in my body, which desires so many things that are anathema to it. How much pain my neshamah must be suffering!"

The soul yearns for Hashem, but it is trapped in this earthly body with its material needs and desires. We should bear this in mind and be more considerate of our *neshamah.*

כִּי עִם ה׳ הַחֶסֶד וְהַרְבֵּה עִמּוֹ פְדוּת
For with Hashem is chesed, and with Him is abundant redemption.

The Midrash says that when Moses ascended to heaven, Hashem

showed him various treasures containing the rewards for the righteous. "This one is for those who studied Torah, and this one is for those who gave *tzedakah* [charity]."

Moses asked, "And this one?"

Hashem replied, "This one is for those who have no merits. 'I shall show favor when I choose to show favor, and I shall show mercy when I choose to show mercy'" (*Exodus* 33:19). Thus, the Talmud tells us, Hashem's *chesed* is boundless, and He shows favor even to those who may be undeserving.

This is an uplifting thought for those who feel themselves *mima'amakim*, in the lowest of depths. We can always look to Hashem with hope.

נַפְשִׁי לַאדֹנָי מִשֹּׁמְרִים לַבֹּקֶר שֹׁמְרִים לַבֹּקֶר
I yearn for Hashem, like the watchmen
who long for the dawn.

The Maggid of Mohilov said that the Talmud states that the night is divided into three shifts of watchmen. The men of the first shift are anxious lest their replacements do not show up on time and they must remain on duty longer. So it is with the guards on the second shift, who worry that their replacements may be tardy. Not so with the third shift. They are free at the dawn, which is never delayed.

This is how secure we are with Hashem. We know his salvation is as certain to come on time as is the dawn.

Blessings of the Shema

Eternal Light

אוֹר עוֹלָם בְּאוֹצַר חַיִּים אוֹרוֹת מֵאֹפֶל אָמַר וַיֶּהִי

The primeval light is in the treasury of eternal life;
'Let there be lights from the darkness,"
He declared — and so it was!

The Talmud (*Chagigah* 12a) says that the initial light of Creation was so bright that with it one could see the entire world, but because Hashem knew that there would be those who would not deserve to see it, He concealed it until the future. Torah commentaries say that Hashem concealed this wonderful light in the Torah.

We all see the world. Some people see the world as a place to have their desires satisfied; those individuals seek to maximize pleasure and fun. Such people are indeed what science calls *homo sapiens*, intelligent hominoids who use their intellect to gratify their wants. The ability to perceive the eternal light enables man to have a true perspective of the world as a place where one can develop his unique spiritual potential. This is accomplished by studying the Torah.

The *berachah* for the Torah includes the words, "Hashem ... implanted eternal life within us." The secular world uses light only to advance its physical needs and wants. From the Torah perspective, this is darkness. The primeval light of Creation is found in the Torah, the "treasury of eternal life." In the future, when "The earth will be as filled with knowledge of Hashem as water covering the seabed" (*Isaiah* 11:9), the primeval light will be returned to mankind.

Chazzan's Repetition of the Amidah (first day)

Based on the tradition ....

The *chazzan* prays, "Based on the tradition of our wise and discerning teachers, and the teaching derived from the knowledge of the discerning, I open my mouth in prayer and supplications to beseech and beg favor before the King Who reigns over kings and the Master of masters."

As was noted earlier, there was dissension among Torah authorities regarding the insertion of *piyutim* into the *Amidah*. Our practice, following the opinion of Rema (*Orach Chaim* 68, 112), is to include numerous *piyutim*; the *chazzan* therefore makes a declaration that we do so by virtue of the authority of our wise and discerning Torah scholars. This is to assure the congregation that these additions are in full accord with Torah authority.

יָרֵאתִי בִּפְצוֹתִי שִׂיחַ לְהַשְׁחִיל
I am frightened as I open my mouth
to bring forth words [of prayer]....

The first *piyut* was composed by R' Yekusiel bar Moshe of Speyer, Germany, in the 11th century. Essentially, it requests God's *reshus* (permission), as it were, to serve as the intercessor of the congregation in bringing their prayers before Hashem.

The *chazzan* experiences a sense of trepidation, aware of his awesome responsibility. He expresses his feelings of inadequacy for this weighty assignment, and asks Hashem to assist him in performing it. We essentially do this for ourselves before every *Amidah,* when we say, "Hashem, open my lips, that my mouth may declare Your praise" (*Psalms* 51:17).

The Torah tells us that on Yom Kippur, the High Priest prays for forgiveness for himself and for his household before praying for atonement for the sins of *Klal Yisrael* (*Leviticus* 16:6). Here, too, the *chazzan* effaces himself and invokes the precedent of Moses interceding on behalf of Israel.

We realize how impoverished we are as we stand before the Infinite One. Yet we may find some comfort in the prayer of *Nishmas,* in which there seems to be an apparent contradiction. It reads, "Were our mouth as full of song as the sea, and our tongue as full of joyous song as its multitude of waves, and our lips as full of praise as the breadth of the heavens, and our eyes as brilliant as the sun and the moon, and our hands as outspread as eagles of the sky and our feet as swift as hinds — we still could not thank You sufficiently ...." Shortly thereafter, we say, "Therefore, the organs that You set within us, and the spirit and soul that You breathed into our nostrils, and the tongue that You placed in our mouth — all of them shall thank and bless ... Your Name, our King." Doesn't this contradict what we just said?

This seeming contradiction can be resolved with a parable:

A king wished to visit a city in his kingdom and sent his ministers to arrange accommodations. They approached someone to host the king. He was overjoyed at the great honor, but expressed his profound concern. "How can I ever provide adequately for His Majesty? Whatever I do will fall far short of what is appropriate for His Majesty!"

The ministers assured him, "You have no need to be concerned. We will bring all the provisions from the palace."

Similarly, we say to Hashem, "We know that there is no way we can adequately address You. However, we have the provisions that You Yourself have given us, 'the organs that You set within us'; we will use those to address You."

אֶת חֵיל יוֹם פְּקֻדָּה

The dread of the remembrance day ....

The second *piyut, Aws Chil,* was composed by R' Elazar HaKalir; it can be seen as the congregation's response to the *chazzan's* "*Yareisi.*" The poet refers to the patriarch Abraham, not only to invoke his merits, but also because Abraham pleaded for the welfare of the most sinful city, Sodom, speaking boldly to Hashem, "Shall the Judge of all the earth not do justice?" (*Genesis* 18:25).

HaKalir refers to a Midrash that relates that Hashem had considered creating Abraham as the first human being, but postponed his birth for twenty generations, so that Abraham might rectify the moral degeneration of the wicked generations that preceded him.

Had Abraham not been born at that time, no one coming later could have achieved that rectification. The poet invokes the merits of Abraham, Sarah, and Isaac to plea for Hashem's mercy for their descendants.

The Ark is opened prior to the recitation of the following *piyut* which is recited on both days of Rosh Hashanah.

אַתָּה הוּא אֱלֹקֵינוּ
Only You Are Our God

Earlier we noted that that R' Chanina overheard someone praising Hashem lavishly, using many superlative adjectives. When he finished, R' Chanina said, "Well, have you exhausted all the praises due to Hashem?"

Many of the *piyutim* do list numerous praises of Hashem. In order to avoid R' Chanina's criticism, some *piyutim* follow the order of the *alef-beis*. Thus, when the *piyut* ends, it is not because one has no further praise of Hashem, but rather because there are only twenty-two letters in the *alef-beis*.

הוּא שָׂח וַיֶּהִי, וְצִוָּה וְנִבְרָאוּ
He spoke and it came into being;
He ordered and they were created.

Similarly, the verses of praise in the Shacharis service are introduced by the *Baruch She'amar* prayer, "Blessed is He Who spoke and the world came into being."

A secular person may not believe that Hashem created the world, but that the universe is spontaneous, having come into existence with "a big bang," although he fails to explain the source of the substrate that enabled the big bang. A world that was not created but "just happened" has no purpose to its existence, and there is no sense in a person having an ultimate purpose in life if there is no purpose to the world.

The belief that Hashem created the world is, of course, fundamental to Judaism. Hence, on Rosh Hashanah, we emphasize this basic concept.

נֵאְפָּד נְקָמָה
He is garbed in vengeance.

How are we to deal with this? We are told to emulate Hashem's Attributes; just as He is merciful and compassionate, we should be merciful and compassionate (*Shabbos* 133b). Yet the Torah forbids us to be vengeful (*Leviticus* 19:18), and the Talmud has the highest commendation for one who does not react with vengance to an offense (*Yoma* 23a).

The answer lies in a Talmudic statement, "A Torah scholar [defending the honor of the Torah] should be as vengeful as a serpent" (*Yoma* 22b). Whereas other animals kill for food, the serpent itself gains nothing by killing someone. The serpent is simply carrying out judgment on one who was sentenced to death. It has no vested interest.

The Talmud says that a Torah scholar may be vengeful in reacting to an offense against the Torah *only if he can be as devoid of personal interest as a snake*. Inasmuch as it is extremely rare for someone to set aside personal interests and to act purely *leshem Shamayim* (in the interest of Hashem), a person should not be vengeful.

There is thus a major qualitative difference between human vengeance and Hashem's vengeance. Hashem has no needs, no personal interest. Hashem's vengeance is absolutely pure, intended for the good of the world. No human being can possibly emulate that.

סִתְרוֹ יֹשֶׁר, עֲצָתוֹ אֱמוּנָה, פְּעֻלָּתוֹ אֱמֶת

His concealment is uprightness;
His advice is faith;
His accomplishment is truth.

Moses said, "The Rock! — perfect is His work, for all His paths are justice; a God of faith without iniquity, righteous and fair is He" (*Deuteronomy* 32:4). To our human perception, many things seem unfair. It is therefore an act of faith to assert that everything Hashem does is just and upright.

His uprightness is concealed from us, and so we must have faith that everything Hashem does is in the interest of truth, for only Hashem knows the complete truth.

☞ *Eternal Reign*

The Ark is opened when this *piyut* is recited.

ה׳ מֶלֶךְ, ה׳ מָלָךְ, ה׳ יִמְלֹךְ לְעוֹלָם וָעֶד

Hashem Reigns, Hashem Has Reigned,
Hashem Shall Reign for Eternity

As was noted earlier, this verse does not appear in Scripture, but was formulated by the Sages incorporating segments of Scriptural verses.

This *piyut* appears to be a prelude to the *Kedushah,* in which we say, "We [Israel] shall sanctify Your Name in this world, just as they [the angels] sanctify it in heaven above…. And one [angel] will call another and say, 'Holy, Holy, Holy ….'" This *piyut* thus describes how both the angels and Israel declare aloud Hashem's reign in the present, past, and future. The triple formulation of this *piyut* corresponds to the threefold evocation, "Holy, Holy, Holy," of the *Kedushah.*

. This *piyut* is generally read responsively, but in some synagogues the congregation joins the *chazzan* to chant the *piyut* in unison.

It is not always clear whether the author is referring to the angels or to Israel. Thus, the phrase, "Those wise in spiritual mysteries," which appears later in the *piyut,* could apply to both.

A *piyut* found in the Yom Kippur service states that Hashem prefers the adoration of mortals to that of angels. The kabbalistic writings point out that because mortals must strive to attain spirituality, they are superior to angels, which are created as spiritual beings.

☞ *The Merciful Judge*

וּבְכֵן לְךָ הַכֹּל יַכְתִּירוּ׃ לְקֵל עוֹרֵךְ דִּין

And So, All Shall Ascribe the Crown to You:
To God Who prepares man for judgment ….

This *piyut* is recited by some congregations during Shacharis of the first day of Rosh Hashanah, and during Mussaf of the second day.

In the Talmud (*Avodah Zarah* 4a) there is a dispute as to the exact time that Hashem judges the world, whether it is early in the day or at a somewhat later hour. By reciting the *piyut* during Shacharis of the first day and during Mussaf of the second day, we accommodate both opinions.

This *piyut* describes the attributes whereby Hashem can exercise His mercy and compassion (*rachamim*) for Israel even within the stern parameters of strict judgment (*din*). For example, we say "The One Who forgives sins in judgment (*din*)," but it would appear that the forgiveness of sins is by virtue of *rachamim* rather than *din*.

Bnei Yisaschar has an ingenious explanation. In the recitation of *Selichos*, we quote the prophet, "'Come, let us reason together,' says Hashem, 'If your sins are like scarlet they will become white as snow; if they have become red as crimson, they will become [white] as wool.'" (*Isaiah* 1:18). *Bnei Yisaschar* comments that when a plaintiff calls a defendant to a trial before a judge, it is because he expects to win. Here, Hashem is calling Israel to trial, saying, "Come to trial, and you will be forgiven." Is it not strange to call a defendant to trial so that he (the defendant) will emerge exonerated?

Bnei Yisaschar explains that Hashem rules the world according to the principles of justice, as it says in *Proverbs* 29:4, "Through justice a king establishes a land ...." That is why the Talmud denounces anyone who says that Hashem will overlook one's sins. It is not a matter of "overlooking." There is forgiveness, and forgiveness must fall within the framework of justice. A person is forgiven when he deserves to be forgiven. If a person does sincere *teshuvah*, and, as the Rambam says, changes his character so that he will no longer sin, then he is essentially a different person, one who cannot be held culpable for the person he had once been, the person who committed the transgression. This is justice, but simply overlooking sins, without *teshuvah*, as though they had not occurred, is not justice, and it is not Hashem's way to do that.

However, Hashem desires to forgive our sins, and if a person has not done proper *teshuvah*, Hashem seeks to find a way to forgive him that will not violate the principles of justice. Therefore, Hashem calls us to a *din Torah* (court of Jewish law) in which He is the plaintiff and we are the defendants. The halachah states that if a wealthy person and a poor person come to a *din Torah*, each must appear to the judge to be of equal stature. If the wealthy person is wearing an expensive suit and the poor person is in tattered clothes, the judge may be drawn to favor the more attractive litigant. The poor person cannot afford fine clothes. Therefore, Torah law requires that the judge tell the wealthy person, "Either buy the poor person a fine suit such as yours or wear tattered clothing like his."

Since Hashem calls us to the *din Torah*, we must appear to be equal, as it were. Sins are referred to as "crimson garments," and we approach the *din Torah* garbed in these. Clearly Hashem is absolute purity, and obviously He cannot be clothed in the crimson garments of sin. The only alternative is that we be divested of our crimson garments and be pure as well, which can happen only if our sins are forgiven. By calling us to a *din Torah*, which requires abiding by halachah, Hashem enables us to be forgiven for our sins without violating the absolute principles of justice.

That is what is meant by *rachum badin*. Hashem finds a way to be merciful while remaining within the bounds of *din*. This is why we say on Rosh Hashanah and Yom Kippur, "*l'Mochel avonos badin* — to the One Who forgives sins in judgment."

לְבוֹחֵן לְבָבוֹת בְּיוֹם דִּין

To the One Who tests hearts on the day of judgment ....

Yaavetz relates that during the Inquisition, when Jews were forced to renounce Hashem or be put to death, there were some Jews who had not been at all Torah observant, yet they elected to die rather than to forsake their faith. R' Shneur Zalman in *Tanya* says that there is a nucleus of love for Hashem in every Jew, regardless of whether he observes Torah; this vital force is a bequest from the patriarch Abraham. When put to the test, this nucleus of loving faith rises to the surface and the Jew declares his devotion to Hashem.

On the Day of Judgment, Hashem looks into the heart of every Jew, and sees the indestructible nucleus of love for Him.

לְקוֹנֶה עֲבָדָיו בַּדִּין

To the One Who acquires His servants
— in judgment ....

There is a Chassidic story regarding this verse.

> *R' Levi Yitzchak of Berditchev was the advocate par excellence for Klal Yisrael.*
>
> *One Rosh Hashanah, R' Levi Yitzchak saw that Satan had brought heaps of Jewish sins before the Heavenly Throne. He said to Satan, "Is that all you*

have? Why, there are many more sins that you've left behind. Go fetch them."

Satan left the mound of sins, and was able to find only a few more that he had overlooked. In his absence, R' Levi Yitzchak took the collection of sins and threw them to the bottom of the sea.

When Satan returned and saw that the sins were gone, he searched for the thief who had stolen them, and discovered that it was R' Levi Yitzchak. Satan then brought R' Levi Yitzchak to trial before the Heavenly tribunal. The court ruled that he must pay for his theft. Inasmuch as he had no way of paying, they applied the rule that a thief who cannot pay must be sold into servitude (Exodus 22:2). They looked for a buyer, and Hashem said, "I will buy him."

This is why the *piyut* refers to "The One Who acquires His servants — in judgment."

לְקוֹנֶה עֲבָדָיו בַּדִּין, לְרַחֵם עַמּוֹ בְּיוֹם דִּין
To the One Who acquires His servants — in judgment;
To the One Who is merciful to His people —
on the day of judgment ....

R' Moshe Leib of Sasov explained the juxtaposition of these two verses with the Talmudic statement, "One who acquires a Jewish servant is as though he acquires a master over himself" (*Kiddushin* 20a), because he must provide the servant with all the comforts he himself enjoys.

"Master of the Universe!" R' Moshe Leib declared, "You have acquired us as Your servants [*Leviticus* 25:55]. Halachah requires that You provide us with all our needs."

☞ *Our Father Is Our King*

אָבִינוּ מַלְכֵּנוּ
Our Father, Our King

The Talmud relates that once when there was a drought in Eretz Yisrael, the community held special prayers for rain, led by the great sage, R' Eliezer. When there was no response to the prayers, R' Akiva, a disciple of R' Eliezer, submitted several supplications beginning with the words *Avinu Malkeinu* (Our Father, our King), and it began to rain. This potent prayer was expanded and is recited during the Ten Days of Repentance and on communal fast days.

It is of interest that the Talmud (*Taanis* 25b) explains that R' Akiva was not a greater Torah scholar than his master, R' Eliezer. The reason that R' Akiva's prayers were answered is because R' Akiva did not take umbrage when someone offended him, and was quick to grant forgiveness.

The prayer, *Avinu Malkeinu,* reminds us how important it is that we do not harbor resentment against those who may have provoked us, and that we should readily forgive them. This makes our prayers more propitious.

We should at all times bear in mind our dual relationship to Hashem, as both His subjects and His children.

In the Maariv prayer, *Hashkiveinu,* we say, "*Hashkiveinu Hashem Elokeinu* — Lay us down to sleep, Hashem, our God. Some *siddurim* read, *"Hashkiveinu Avinu* — Lay us down to sleep, our Father. It seems a bit bold to ask of Hashem as King to lay us down to sleep, but it is perfectly appropriate to ask this of a Father.

חָטָאנוּ לְפָנֶיךָ

... we have sinned before You.

(Note: Following the teachings of the Ari *z"l,* some people omit those verses that refer to sin on Rosh Hashanah.)

אֵין לָנוּ מֶלֶךְ אֶלָּא אַתָּה

... we have no King but You.

How can we ask Hashem to forgive our sins? We have sinned against Him, and the halachah is that a king may not forgive an offense against him (*Kesubos* 17a).

A king may not forgive an affront against him because, in addition to being a personal offense, it is also an indignity against the crown. Inasmuch as other kings will occupy that office, a king may not forgive an offense that will affect his successors' honor.

That is why we say, "We have no King but You." Hashem is the only King we will ever have, and since there will be no other kings whose honor He must protect, He can forgive our sins.

The Maggid of Ratzki related a parable.

> *A troop was commanded to go to a northern army base, where everything had been prepared for them. However, the sergeant in command had plans of his own, and he*

directed the troops to a southern base. When the troops arrived there, they found the barracks in disrepair and there was no food in the kitchen.

A messenger then arrived, with orders from the irate general to promptly reverse course and march to the northern base. The troops bound the sergeant in chains and turned around. They told the messenger, "Tell the general we're on the way back. This misguided sergeant misled us. We are loyal to the general and will obey his orders."

Similarly, Hashem gave us instructions on how to live. The *yetzer hara*, acting as though it had authority, compelled us to deviate from Hashem's orders, and we realize how badly we had been misled. We have deposed the *yetzer hara* and we now declare our loyalty to Hashem, promising to follow His orders: "Our Father, Our King, we have no King but You."

עֲשֵׂה עִמָּנוּ לְמַעַן שְׁמֶךָ

... deal [kindly] with us for Your Name's sake.

Another parable from the Maggid of Ratzki:

A traveler came to a small town and entered a watchmaker's shop. He was surprised to find that the craftsman had produced excellent timepieces, elaborately fashioned and fit for royalty, but no one in the town appreciated his work.

When the traveler returned to the city, he told of the watchmaker's unusual timepieces, and he repeated the

*incident wherever he went. Soon the watchmaker began to
serve elite customers, for whom he designed unique watches
and clocks. His fame spread far and wide, and eventually
he was asked to design a custom-made clock for the palace.*

*When the traveler returned to the small town,
he asked the watchmaker to repair his wristwatch.
The watchmaker said, "What a chutzpah! I design
timepieces for the king and the nobility, and you are
asking me to fix your wristwatch?"*

*The traveler said, "Just one minute. You were once
totally unknown. I was the one who told people about
you. You serve the king and nobility because I spread
your name far and wide. You owe me this courtesy."*

So, too, we say to Hashem, "Before our patriarch Abraham, the
world did not know of You. It was our ancestor who made Your
Name known all over the world. In his merit, we deserve that you
should deal kindly with us."

בַּטֵּל מֵעָלֵינוּ כָּל גְּזֵרוֹת קָשׁוֹת
… nullify all harsh decrees upon us.

*During the lifetime of the Maggid of Mezeritch, there
were no harsh anti-Semitic decrees in Russia, but these
were reinstated after his death. One of the Maggid's
disciples wondered, "Inasmuch as tzaddikim are even
greater after their death than during their lifetime,
and if the Maggid could forestall evil decrees in his
lifetime, why is he not doing so in Gan Eden?"*

The Maggid appeared to him in a dream and said,
"During my lifetime, with my human perception, I
saw things as bad. I therefore intervened to annul
them. Now, from my perspective in Gan Eden, I see the
ultimate good in them, so I cannot intervene to cancel
them. You still see things with human perception; you
can pray to cancel them."

True, we believe that Hashem does only good, but when we
see things as bad, we have the right to pray that they be eradicated.

סְתוֹם פִּיּוֹת מַשְׂטִינֵנוּ וּמְקַטְרִיגֵנוּ
... seal the mouths of our adversaries and accusers.

Following the horrific Chmielnicki pogroms of 1648, R' Yom
Tov Lipman Heller (author of *Tosafos Yom Tov*) said that it was
revealed to him in a dream that these disasters were a punishment
for conversing during the *davening* and the reading of the Torah.

There were, at that time, some non-observant Jews who vio-
lated Shabbos and did not observe the laws of *kashrus*, both major
Scriptural sins. Why was the onus placed on conversing during
davening?

The Chofetz Chaim cited the Talmud stating that when a person sins, he creates an accusing angel (*Ethics of the Fathers* 4:13).
The angel resulting from the sin bears the characteristic of that
transgression. Thus, the sin of eating non-kosher food or violating
Shabbos does not involve speech, so the accusing angels produced
by these sins are mute and cannot bring charges against the trans-
gressor. However, conversing during *davening* involves speech,

and the angels produced thereby can bring charges citing *all* the person's sins. Similarly, speaking *lashon hara* (defamatory speech), lying, and other sins involving speech create accusatory angels that can bring charges against the sinner.

We pray that Hashem seal the mouths of our accusers. We must be cautious not to create more accusers.

סְלַח וּמְחַל לְכָל עֲוֹנוֹתֵינוּ

... forgive and pardon all our iniquities.

מְחֵה וְהַעֲבֵר פְּשָׁעֵינוּ וְחַטֹּאתֵינוּ מִנֶּגֶד עֵינֶיךָ

*... wipe away and remove our willful sins
and errors from Your sight.*

These verses are not redundant, because there are several levels of forgiveness. One level of forgiveness mandates that the person will not be punished for his sin, but the sin is retained on record, and may later be recalled. This is what happened in reference to the sin of the Golden Calf. Although Hashem forgave the sin and did not destroy the nation, the sin remained on record, and it can contribute its weight to punishments for future sins (*Exodus* 32:34).

A second level of forgiveness is attained when the record is expunged and the sin erased as though it had never happened.

The degree of forgiveness one merits is dependent upon the quality of his *teshuvah*. The more sincere and thorough the *teshuvah*, the more absolute the degree of forgiveness. We ask that Hashem wipe our slates clean, but in order to merit this, our *teshuvah* must be complete.

We might ask, wouldn't it have been more appropriate to recite this verse at the beginning of the *Avinu Malkeinu,* right after we said "We have sinned before You"? Why do we postpone asking for forgiveness until after we have asked for protection from our enemies?

The Maggid of Ratzki related a parable.

> *A father warned his young son not to go outdoors because the streets were covered with ice and extremely slippery. The child disobeyed, went outdoors, and indeed slipped, sustaining a bruise. He came to his father, and said, "I'm sorry I disobeyed you," and asked for something to relieve his pain.*
>
> *However, had he broken his leg when he slipped on the ice, he would not begin by saying, "I'm sorry for disobeying you." He would scream loudly for help. Only after his broken leg was taken care of would he express his remorse for not obeying his father.*

So it is with us. We are in such great danger from all our enemies that we first pray to Hashem to help us, and afterward we say we regret having disobeyed Him.

מְחוֹק בְּרַחֲמֶיךָ הָרַבִּים כָּל שִׁטְרֵי חוֹבוֹתֵינוּ

... erase through Your abundant compassion
all records of our guilt.

Inasmuch as we have just prayed, "forgive and pardon all our iniquities," what are we asking for with the words, "erase through Your abundant compassion all records of our guilt"?

A more accurate translation is, "Erase all our contracts of indebtedness." The Chofetz Chaim explains that in addition to the sins we have committed, we are also culpable for the sins others have committed, if we had the ability to prevent them. The term "contracts of indebtedness" refers to those sins of others for which we are held accountable, and we ask Hashem to erase these contracts of indebtedness.

שְׁלַח רְפוּאָה שְׁלֵמָה לְחוֹלֵי עַמֶּךָ
... send complete recovery to the sick of Your people.

This is a rather unusual expression. In the *Amidah* we say, "Heal us, Hashem, and we shall be healed." Why use the expression "*send* complete recovery"?

The Torah specifies that one who is sick should avail himself of treatment (*Exodus* 21:19). We pray that Hashem should provide us with the right *shaliach* (emissary) to carry out His healing. Therefore, we say "*send* complete recovery," i.e., guide us to the agent through whom You will heal us.

כָּתְבֵנוּ בְּסֵפֶר פַּרְנָסָה וְכַלְכָּלָה
... inscribe us in the book of sustenance and support.

The Talmud says that a person's earnings are determined on Rosh Hashanah (Beitzah 16b).

A student of the Baal Shem Tov asked him to explain the apparent contradiction to the Talmudic statement that a person is judged each day (Rosh Hashanah 16a). "How can these two statements be reconciled?" the student asked.

The Baal Shem Tov glanced through the window and

saw Chaikel, the water carrier, carrying two buckets of water. He beckoned to him and asked, "How are things with you, Chaikel?"

"Not good," Chaikel said. "At my age, I still have to shlep buckets of water up the hill to support myself."

Several days later, the Baal Shem Tov again saw Chaikel. "How are things with you?" he asked.

Chaikl responded, "Rebbe, I can't complain. If at my age I can still shlep buckets of water up the hill, I'm thankful to Hashem."

The Baal Shem Tov said to his student, "Both Talmudic statements are correct. On Rosh Hashanah it was decreed that Chaikel should earn his living as a water carrier. How Chaikel accepts this decree can vary from day to day."

כָּתְבֵנוּ בְּסֵפֶר זְכֻיּוֹת
... inscribe us in the book of merits

How can we ask this of Hashem? If we have merits, He will certainly inscribe us in the book of merits. If we do not, how can we ask Him to do so?

The Talmud says that if one does *teshuvah* out of love for Hashem, his sins are converted into merits (*Yoma* 86b). Inasmuch as we have asked Hashem, "Return us to You in perfect repentance," requesting that He help us do sincere *teshuvah*, our sins will be converted into merits, and we can thus be inscribed in the book of merits.

הַצְמַח לָנוּ יְשׁוּעָה בְּקָרוֹב
… make salvation sprout for us soon.

The seeds of the Ultimate Redemption were planted long ago with the Divine promise of *Mashiach*. These seeds have taken root as a result of the Torah and mitzvos of Jews throughout history. For the salvation to blossom, we must continue to nourish the plant with Torah and mitzvos.

הָרֵם קֶרֶן יִשְׂרָאֵל עַמֶּךָ
… raise high the pride of Israel, Your People.

The word *keren*, translated as "pride," has another meaning as well. If one invests money for a profitable return, the principal is referred to as *keren*, and the profit is *revach*.

The Maggid cites the Talmud, "Hashem did not exile the Jews among the nations for any reason other than to attract converts" (*Pesachim* 87b). Thus, Hashem "invested" the Jews among the nations in order to reap a profit. The Maggid said that we pray, "Our Father, Our King, lift the *keren*, the principal, out of exile. The investment is not working; You are losing principal instead of making profit."

מַלֵּא יָדֵינוּ מִבִּרְכוֹתֶיךָ
… fill our hands from Your blessings.

When I was a child, my mother would tell me bedtime stories. I had no idea that she was preparing me for my career, and only decades later did I realize the point of the following story.

A poor man prayed to God for wealth. One day, he awoke to find a purse near his bed. The purse contained one dollar, and when he removed the dollar, another dollar appeared in its place. He was overjoyed by his good fortune, and kept on pulling out dollar after dollar. Three days later, he was found dead, lying on a huge pile of dollars.

That is the story of addiction to anything. There is never an end-point at which one feels one has had enough. The persistent drive for even more is ultimately fatal. In forty years of treating addicts, I realized the truth in my mother's bedtime story.

Addiction to anything is a bottomless pit.

We have prayed, "Our Father, our King. Inscribe us in the book of sustenance and support." We add to this the prayer that Hashem should fill our hands with His blessings; i.e., that we should feel satiated and not drive ourselves to destruction with insatiable pursuits.

פְּתַח שַׁעֲרֵי שָׁמַיִם לִתְפִלָּתֵנוּ
... open the gates of heaven to our prayer.

Hashem has said, "Open for Me a portal the size of a point of a needle, and I will open for you a portal through which wagons can pass" (*Shir HaShirim Rabbah* 5:3).

A house caught fire, and people rushed to save the dwellers, who were shouting, "Help! Save us."

But the door was locked from the inside, and the people shouted back, "Open the door! Turn the key and we'll save you!"

We ask Hashem, "Open the gates of heaven."
Hashem's response is, "Turn the key from inside. Open
for Me a portal the size of a point of a needle, and I will
open for you a portal through which wagons can pass."
(Maggid of Ratzki)

חָנֵּנוּ וַעֲנֵנוּ, כִּי אֵין בָּנוּ מַעֲשִׂים, עֲשֵׂה עִמָּנוּ צְדָקָה וָחֶסֶד וְהוֹשִׁיעֵנוּ

... be gracious with us and answer us, though we
have no worthy deeds; treat us with charity
and kindness, and save us.

The Maggid of Dubnow explained this verse with a parable about a customer who orders a great deal of merchandise, then says to the shopkeeper, "I don't have the money to pay for this. Please let me have it on credit."

Similarly, after presenting Hashem a long list of requests, we say, "Please Hashem, we don't have the currency — the worthy deeds or merits — to pay for all that we are asking. Please fulfill our wishes 'on credit,' for the mitzvos that we will do in the future."

Chazzan's Repetition of the Amidah (second day)

*S*hacharis is essentially the same as the first day. There are however, several changes in the *chazzan's* repetition of the *Amidah*.

☞ *Humility*

אָתִיתִי לְחַנְּנָךְ

I come to implore You

This is a declaration of total self-effacement, in which the *chazzan* humbly expresses his inadequacy as a representative of the congregants to bring their prayers to Hashem. Before the invention of the printing press made prayer books available to all, the *chazzan* was indeed the one who chanted the prayers on behalf of the entire congregation and therefore this prayer was decidedly poignant.

Anivus is the finest of all human character traits. Moses was superlative in many aspects, yet the only trait the Torah mentions was that he was "the most humble of people on earth" (*Numbers* 12:3). Humility is so dear to Hashem that He says He makes His presence with the humble (*Isaiah* 57:15).

"I plead for mercy like a beggar at the door." King David uses the rather strange expression, "I am prayer" (*Psalms* 109:4). If a well-dressed person comes to your door, you ask him what he wants. If a person wearing tattered clothes comes to your door, there is no need to ask him what he wants. His appearance speaks for itself. Similarly, David says, "Hashem, just look at me. You can see how needy I am."

A poor person arouses your sympathy, and you offer him something without seeking to know details about him. The Talmud says, "One does not investigate the worthiness of one who asks for food" (*Bava Basra* 9:1).

With this attitude, one is certain to receive mercy from Hashem "A gentle reply turns away wrath" (*Proverbs* 15:1).

שָׁלַחְתִּי
I have been dispatched

The Ark is opened briefly and although the *chazzan* humbles himself, he praises the congregation, saying:

שָׁלַחְתִּי — I have been dispatched on the mission of the treasured company, who observe Your faith and reverently proclaim Your Oneness.

The *Amidah* continues with the same text as that of the first day.

Removal of the Torah from the Ark

☞ The Thirteen Attributes of Mercy

Within weeks of the Revelation at Sinai, the Israelites committed the sin of worshiping the Golden Calf. The Talmud compares this to the unforgivable sin of a bride who is unfaithful during the wedding feast (*Shabbos* 88b). Yet, Moses was able to achieve forgiveness for his people, and Hashem revealed to him the Thirteen Attributes of Mercy, saying that whenever Israel recites these words, Hashem will forgive the nation (*Rosh Hashanah* 17b). *Alshich* says that merely *reciting* the Thirteen Attributes is not enough. We must *perform* them, as the Talmud says, "Just as I am compassionate, you should be compassionate" (*Shabbos* 133b).

There is a charming explanation of a problem posed by two verses following the sin of the Golden Calf. Hashem sends an angel in His stead to lead the Jewish people to the Promised Land. Hashem does this — rather than lead His nation — because they "are a stiff-necked people," in constant danger of sinning and incurring Hashem's wrath. Therefore Hashem chose not to remain in their midst, for He might annihilate them in His anger (*Exodus* 33:3). After Hashem reveals the Thirteen Attributes of Mercy, Moses asks Hashem to be with Israel "for it is a stiff-necked people" (ibid. 34:9). Why would Moses invoke in Israel's favor a trait that Hashem had criticized?

The Maggid of Dubnow answers with another of his inimitable parables.

> *After a day's work, the peddlers would get together to compare how well they had done that day. One peddler complained that he had not made a single sale. "What were you selling?" the other peddlers asked.*
>
> *"Wooden cutlery," he said.*
>
> *"And where were you peddling them?" they asked.*
>
> *"In the affluent neighborhood." he said.*
>
> *The other peddlers laughed at him. "You fool!" they said. "Of course you did not make a sale. Wealthy people have no need for wooden cutlery. They use silver and gold cutlery. You should have been peddling in the poor neighborhoods. **They** can use your wares."*

"Similarly," the Maggid says, "after Hashem revealed His Attributes of Mercy, Slow to Anger, and Forgiver of Iniquity, Moses said, 'What would You do with those Attributes in heaven? Angels are obedient and they do not sin. You cannot implement these Attributes among the heavenly angels. But if You come among us, we are a stiff-necked people, and **we** can use Your wares.'"

The Rebbe of Kotzk lauded this parable, and said that it was indeed the correct explanation of the apparently conflicting verses.

Torah Reading for the First Day

☞ *Genesis 21*

> *Sarah saw the son whom Hagar the Egyptian*
> *had borne to Abraham, mocking (v. 9).*

Malbim notes that the words "borne to Abraham" appear to be superfluous. We know from the previous text that Hagar bore Ishmael to Abraham. Malbim explains why Sarah was so intolerant of Ishmael.

Rashi cites the Midrash that cynics said that Abimelech must be the father of Sarah's child, since she and Abraham had been married for many decades but she had given birth only after having been kidnaped by the Philistine king (Rashi, *Genesis* 25:19). Ishmael, too, had joined the cynics in denying Isaac's paternity. This is what the Torah means when it says "Sarah saw the son whom Hagar the Egyptian *had borne to Abraham, mocking.*" Ishmael was saying that he was the *only* son born to Abraham. This is why Sarah said, "The son of this slavewoman shall not inherit with my son, with

Isaac." (Rashi, *Genesis* 21:9) Ishmael would dispute Isaac's right to inherit, and there was therefore no choice but to banish him.

> *When the water ... was consumed, she cast off the boy beneath one of the trees. She went and sat herself down at a distance ... for she said, 'Let me not see the death of the child'" (vs. 15, 16).*

It is worthwhile to cite the comment of Rabbi Samson Raphael Hirsch.

> Hagar's whole behavior is extremely characteristic and reveals the shortcoming, the imperfection of the Hamitic character. A Jewish mother would not have forsaken her child, even if all she could do would be to try to comfort him, even if it were only to soothe him for a millionth part of a second. To go away, simply because "one cannot bear to see the misery," is not evidence of sympathetic feeling for another, but is the cruel egoism of a human nature that is still crude. In truly humane people, the feelings of duty master the strongest emotions, make one forget one's own painful feelings, and give helpful assistance even if one can do no more than provide the comfort of one's caring presence.

> *For God has heeded the cry of the youth in his present state (v. 17).*

The Midrash states that the angels pleaded with Hashem not

to save Ishmael because his offspring would murder and persecute the Jews. Hashem responded that He would judge Ishmael only in his present state of innocence, and not by what he would do in the future.

Perhaps this is one of the reasons that we read this portion of the Torah on Rosh Hashanah. During the month of Elul, we do *teshuvah* and make various resolutions about refining our character. Unfortunately, although we did this in past years, no sooner did Yom Kippur pass than we regressed to our earlier behavior patterns.

By reading this portion of the Torah, we plead to Hashem that He judge us in our present state of *teshuvah,* just as He judged Ishmael favorably, and not judge us by the likelihood that we will relapse in the future.

Then Hashem opened her eyes and she perceived a well of water (v. 19).

The Torah does not say that Hashem created a well for her, but rather that He enabled her to see what she had failed to see earlier.

This is a most important teaching. If adverse circumstances cause one to panic, one may be oblivious to opportunities and solutions that may be readily at hand. A well had been there all the time, but Hagar panicked and did not see it.

It is not easy to maintain composure under stress. Firm *emunah* (faith; trust) in Hashem will serve to forestall panic. It is always wise to share your anxieties with someone else, who, because he or she is not experiencing your own particular stress, may be able to enlighten you, enabling you to see that which you did not initially perceive.

— 108 —

And the two of them entered a covenant (v. 27).

The Torah is very attentive to its wording, and will not use even one extra letter unnecessarily. The verse could have read, "And *they* entered a covenant," which, of course, would mean that the two of them entered a covenant. Why the superfluous wording?

R' Simchah Bunim of Pshische says that the Torah means to stress that although it was necessary for Abraham to interact with Abimelech, nevertheless Abraham avoided closeness with him. They remained separate even after executing an agreement.

We often interact with people in our environment who are far different from us in their *hashkafah* (philosophy of life). Too intimate a relationship may expose us to concepts that differ from Torah *hashkafah*, and we may open ourselves to becoming vulnerable to alien influences. We may have cordial relationships with others, but we should never forget our uniqueness as Torah Jews.

☞ *The Haftarah of the First Day*

The *haftarah* (*I Samuel* 1:1–2:10) has a similar theme to that of the Torah reading. In the latter, the matriarch Sarah bore a child after having been childless for decades, and in the former, Hannah, too, bore a child only after years of being barren.

The Midrash states that Elkanah would go to the Tabernacle in Shiloh using a different path every year, so that he could inspire the residents of various communities to join him in the pilgrimage. Although women and children are exempt from making the pilgrimage, Elkanah wanted them to experience the Sanctuary in person. He would assemble all of his relations, and they would camp in the center of the towns on the way to Shiloh. When the townspeople asked where they were going, Elkanah explained the significance of visiting the Sanctuary, and he prevailed on many to join him. Hashem said to Elkanah, "You made the effort to bring merits to many Jews. Therefore, you will be blessed with a child who will reinforce *Klal Yisrael* with mitzvos."

Like the matriarchs Sarah, Rebecca, and Rachel, Hannah was childless because Hashem desired her impassioned prayers; not because Hashem needed the prayers of these righteous women, but because they had the awesome responsibility of being the mothers of the Jewish nation. There is no way to develop the loftiest levels of spirituality other than through intense prayer, and this is why Hashem withheld their having children. (Leah had merited her spirituality by virtue of praying that she not be compelled to marry Esau [Rashi, *Genesis* 29:17].)

The Midrash says that Elkanah's second wife, Peninah, had the best of intentions when she provoked Hannah (by asking, for example, "What have you bought for your children?"); her plan was to goad Hannah to intense prayer. Yet Peninah was punished because she told Hannah, "The reason you have no children is because Hashem is punishing you for your sins, and you must do *teshuvah*."

This is an important teaching. When tragedy strikes, there are often some "all-knowing" people who "know" why the misfortune transpired and share their conclusions with the suffering person; this is pouring salt on open wounds. When someone suffers, one should sympathize and truly care, sharing his pain, but not try to explain why Hashem allows tribulations to occur. No one is privy to Hashem's reasoning.

There is an important psychological insight derived from the interchange between Hannah and the High Priest, Eli. The Talmud states that Hannah prayed to Hashem for "an average child, not too tall nor too short, not too bright but not dull. "When she said to Eli, "This is the child for whom I prayed," she meant, "I received what I prayed for, an average child — not too bright, but not too dull" (*Berachos* 31b).

R' Chaim Shmulevitz says, "Think of it! The prophet Samuel, who is considered to be on a level with Moses and Aaron combined, was of just average potential!" (*Sichos Mussar* 5731:18). If we refrain from developing ourselves to the highest levels of spirituality, it is simply because we do not exert the effort to do so.

When we read the biographies of *tzaddikim*, we may say, "Well, you can't expect me to be a Chofetz Chaim." But why not? The Chofetz Chaim was not born a complete *tzaddik*. He achieved his greatness only by intense effort. Indeed, Rambam says that every person has the capacity to be a *tzaddik* of the caliber of Moses Rabbeinu.

Virtually all the laws of the *Amidah* are derived from Hannah's mode of praying.

Hannah prayed silently, and Eli reprimanded her, mistaking her inaudible mumbling for a symptom of intoxication. When he realized his error, Eli apologized and blessed her. The Talmud says this teaches us that if one accuses another person falsely, he should apologize and bless him.

The Talmud says, "Judge everyone favorably" (*Ethics of the Fathers* 1:6). It is so easy to jump to erroneous conclusions.

> *R' Aryeh Levin joined a funeral procession, and noticed*
> *that a close friend of the deceased left the procession*

*to purchase a flowerpot. R' Levin felt that this was
disrespectful, and reprimanded the man.*

*The man explained, "My friend died of a very
contagious disease, and the doctors said that everything
he had come in contact with must be destroyed. I pleaded
with them not to destroy the tefillin, and I promised that
I would see to it that the tefillin were disposed of safely. I
bought the flowerpot because the halachah requires that
tefillin be buried in an earthenware container. I intend
to bury them in the cemetery."*

*R' Levin apologized profusely and said, "I will never
again suspect a person of wrongdoing without first
investigating the reason for his behavior."*

Hashem impoverishes and makes rich. He humbles and He exalts (I Samuel 2:7).

My father often cited the verse, "May only goodness and kindness pursue me all the days of my life" (*Psalms* 23:6), and asked, "To 'pursue' someone connotes to reach him in order to punish him. Does one 'pursue' someone with goodness and kindness?" My father answered with a parable.

*During a parade, a protestor threw a rock at the king.
The officers seized him and were going to punish him
severely, but the king intervened, and instead of a
punishment, gave the perpetrator a position in the palace.*

*The protestor felt very guilty. "I threw a rock at the
king, and he is so kind to me."*

A bit later, the king promoted him, and his remorse increased. As the king continued to advance his position, he felt progressively more guilt for his act. He felt much worse than he would have had he been punished by imprisonment.

So, my father said, one can punish with kindness. This is what David says to Hashem in the psalm. "If You must pursue me, do so with goodness and kindness."

Hannah, too, expressed this idea by stating, "He humbles and He exalts"; i.e., He can humble someone by exalting him.

We are told that we should thank Hashem for His kindnesses of the past, and ask for His continued *chesed* in the future, just as Hannah did.

☞ *Hannah's Song*

It is of interest that Hannah prayed for the future, not her own, but that of her child:

> Hashem, may those who contend with him be shattered, against each of them let the heavens thunder, may Hashem judge to the ends of the earth, may he give power to his king, and raise the pride of his anointed (*I Samuel* 2:10).

Some interpret the pronouns "him, he, his" in this verse to refer to Hashem. Abarbanel interprets them as referring to Samuel, which is why they appear here in lower case.

"May those who contend with him be shattered." These words refer to the Philistines, as she said, "The bow of the mighty is broken" (ibid. 2:4).

— 113 —

"Let the heavens thunder." May Hashem come to the defense of Israel and frighten away Israel's enemies. Hannah also prophesied that Samuel would pray for thunder when Israel requested a king (*I Samuel* Chapter 12).

"May he give power to his king." This refers to Saul, whom Samuel anointed.

"May he raise the pride of his anointed." The Hebrew word for "pride" is *keren,* which also means "horn." Samuel anointed David with "a horn of oil" (ibid. 16:13); and the Talmud states that anointing with a "horn of oil" rather than with a "flask of oil" symbolized that David's dynasty would be eternal (*Megillah* 14). Thus, Hannah's prayer was that the king anointed by Samuel should head an eternal dynasty.

Hannah teaches us how parents should pray for their children.

> *I cannot refrain from sharing a personal story with you. My mother used to tell me that when I took my first steps, everyone was overjoyed. They clapped their hands and said, "Dos kind geht!" (The child is walking).*
>
> *A meshulach (charity collector) who was present commented, "Yes, I'm sure that when I began to walk, my parents were happy, too. But today, when people see me walking toward them, they are not happy at all."*
>
> *My mother would say, "When a child begins to walk, parents should pray that people should **always** be happy when they see him/her walking toward them."*

Torah Reading for the Second Day

☞ *Genesis* 22

*T*he account of the *Akeidah* is well known. We read that portion of the Torah during Rosh Hashanah to invoke the merit of Abraham, whose devotion to Hashem was so absolute that he was prepared to part with his beloved son if that was Hashem's word.

Abraham's devotion to Hashem was so great that he did not question Hashem, by asking, "You promised me that I would have offspring through Isaac [see *Genesis* 21:12]. Are You going back on Your word?" In perfect faith, Abraham was ready to make the supreme sacrifice. There are many Midrashim about how Satan tried to deter Abraham from carrying out the sacrifice, but Abraham was steadfast in his determination to obey the will of Hashem.

There is more to the story of the *Akeidah* than Abraham's

willingness to accept Hashem's decree. There are several subtle aspects that indicate the totality of Abraham's devotion to Hashem.

"Abraham woke up early in the morning" (*Genesis* 22:3). The Sages praise Abraham's diligence and enthusiasm to fulfill Hashem's command; he did not delay until later in the day, but arose early in the morning. But there is a hidden message in the words, "Abraham woke up early in the morning." It means *that he slept through the night!* Think of it. A father knows that the next day he has to bring his son as an offering, and it does not disturb his sleep! That is a superhuman feat, to have such faith in Hashem! *Anything Hashem wants is fine with me. Hashem wants me to have a son? That is fine with me. Hashem wants me to give up my son? That, too, is fine with me.* Perfect trust in Hashem allowed him to have equanimity, to sleep peacefully under what would be decidedly unimaginable stress for anyone else. That was the greatness of Abraham.

Another insight to consider is that throughout his adult life, Abraham had been denouncing idol worship, and human sacrifice in particular, which the Torah singles out as an abomination: "For even their sons and their daughters have they burned in the fire for their gods" (*Deuteronomy* 12:31). Abraham knew that Hashem despised human sacrifice, and Hashem's command to sacrifice Isaac went against every fiber of his body. Yet, he unquestioningly accepted the command.

But what would he do when he would encounter the people to whom he had so vehemently denounced human sacrifice? How could he face them? He would have to say to them, "For the past 137 years, I was wrong. You are right, and I was wrong." But Abraham was prepared to do this.

Think for a moment how quick we are to defend our mistakes, and how resistant we are to admit that we made a mistake, and you can then appreciate Abraham's greatness. He was willing to publicly admit that he had been wrong *all his life!* That requires extraordinary courage, and this tells us something of the character of Abraham.

This is relevant to Rosh Hashanah and Yom Kippur when we ask forgiveness for our sins. We can obtain forgiveness only if we own up to our sins. It is not uncommon for people to deny having sinned. It is not that they lie, but that they have rationalized, explained away, and justified their actions. The prophet says, "I am [entering into] judgment with you because of your saying, 'I have not sinned'" (*Jeremiah* 2:35). We must do a careful soul-searching and be willing to admit that we were wrong.

We will not be tested with the likes of the *Akeidah*, but we should be able to strengthen our trust in Hashem and accept whatever happens with equanimity, and we should not hesitate to admit that we were wrong. These are among the lessons we should learn from the *Akeidah*.

☞ *Haftarah for the Second Day*

It is generally assumed that the relevance of this chapter in *Jeremiah* 31:1-19 to Rosh Hashanah is that it contains the verse we recite in *Zichronos,* "Is Ephraim My most precious son or a delightful child, that whenever I speak of him, I remember him more and more? Therefore, My inner self yearns for him, I will surely take pity on him — these are the words of Hashem" (*Jeremiah* 31:19).

There may also be another reason why this chapter is appropriate. The Torah reading evinces the extraordinary *mesiras nefesh* of the patriarch Abraham. What could be greater than the willingness to offer one's beloved son as a sacrificial offering to Hashem? But perhaps there is something greater.

> *The Midrash (Eichah Rabbah) relates that when Jerusalem was destroyed by the Babylonians, much of its population killed, and the Jews of Israel exiled, the patriarch Abraham came before Hashem. "At age one hundred You blessed me with a child. You later told me to bring my beloved child as an offering to You. I did not hesitate, and I was willing to sacrifice my child to You. Is this how You reward me, to see my children killed and exiled?" Hashem did not respond to Abraham.*
>
> *Isaac came before Hashem. "I was thirty-seven years old when my father wanted to bring me as an offering to You. Not only did I not resist, but I even asked my father to bind me securely to the altar, lest I become agitated, move, and disqualify the sacrifice. That was how devoted I was to You. Is this my reward, to see my children killed and exiled?" Hashem did not respond to Isaac.*
>
> *Jacob came before Hashem. "You assigned me the mission to establish the twelve tribes. What suffering I sustained to do so! I had to flee from my brother Esau, who wished to kill me. I spent twenty-two years of misery with the scoundrel Laban, who repeatedly cheated me. I agonized for twenty-two years over the disappearance of my beloved son, Joseph. Never did I lose my faith in You.*

Is this my reward, to see my children killed and exiled?"
Hashem did not respond to Jacob.

Then Moses came before Hashem. "You gave me
the task of taking Your children out of Egypt and
shepherding them through forty years of wandering
in the desert. I carried them on my back like a steed,
tolerating their complaints and bickering. Is this my
reward, to see the people I cared for killed and exiled?"
Hashem did not respond to Moses.

Then the matriarch Rachel came before Hashem.
"You know how much Jacob loved me, and that he
worked seven years for my hand in marriage. I knew
that my father was a scoundrel and that he might
substitute my sister Leah in my place. I gave Jacob a
secret code, so that he could discern if it was me or Leah.
When I saw that my father had indeed set Leah in my
stead for the wedding, I realized that if Jacob made use
of the secret code, Leah would be publicly humiliated.
Therefore, to protect my sister's dignity, I told her the
secret code. I was willing to give up Jacob to my sister,
and see the man I loved married to my sister instead of
me, for what reason? To spare my sister a few moments
of embarrassment. Is this my reward, to see my children
killed and exiled?"

Hashem responded to Rachel, "It is in your merit,
Rachel, that I will yet save your children. 'Restrain your
voice from weeping and your eyes from tears; for there
is a reward for your accomplishment — the words of
Hashem — and they shall return from the enemy's land.

> *There is hope for you ultimately — the words of Hashem — and your children shall return to their border'" (Jeremiah 31:15,16).*
>
> *The pleas of Abraham, Isaac, Jacob, and Moses did not elicit the desired response. Only Rachel's plea aroused Hashem's mercy.*

The sacrifices of the Patriarchs were indeed great, but Rachel was willing to give up an entire lifetime, to spend the rest of her life without the man she loved, to see him married to her sister, and to what purpose? To spare her sister a few moments of embarrassment!

The Torah reading is about the great *mesiras nefesh* of Abraham. The *haftarah* is about Hashem's response to Rachel, whose *mesiras nefesh* was regarded even more favorably.

In conjunction, we learn the reward of living a life in which the will of Hashm has primacy, even when it seems to go against our greatest desires. On Rosh Hashanah, Hashem has been crowned King over all of mankind. His sovereignty is absolute and our recognition of this will enable us to do *teshuvah* out of love for Him.

Teki'as Shofar

The Sounding of the Shofar

☞ *Symbolism of the Shofar*

*R*av Saadiah Gaon enumerates ten symbolic allusions in the mitzvah of shofar, as enumerated in the ArtScroll *Rosh Hashanah Machzor*.

1. Rosh Hashanah marks the anniversary of the day Hashem simultaneously created and became Sovereign of the universe. We blow the shofar since it is customary to sound the trumpets at the coronation of a new king.

2. Just as a king may proclaim a period of amnesty before he punishes wrongdoers, so the shofar blast proclaims, "Whoever wishes to repent — let him do so now. If not, let him not complain later."

3. At Mount Sinai, when the Jews accepted the Torah, the sound of the shofar continually increased and was very great (*Exodus* 19:19). On Rosh Hashanah the shofar reminds us to renew that commitment.

4. The shofar reminds us of the admonitions of the prophets and their calls to repentance — as is stated (*Ezekiel* 33:2-3): "When I bring a sword upon a land ... [the sentry] blows the shofar and warns the people."

5. The shofar reminds us to pray for the rebuilding of the destroyed Holy Temple, of which the prophet lamented: "I shall not be silent, for the sound of the shofar have you heard, O my soul, the shout of war. Destruction upon destruction has been proclaimed" (*Jeremiah* 4:19-20).

6. The shofar, a ram's horn, reminds us of *Akeidas Yitzchak,* the Binding of Isaac (*Genesis* 22), when Abraham sacrificed a ram in lieu of his son. Thus, may our remembrances ascend before Him for the good.

7. The sound of the shofar inspires fear and trembling in the hearts of all who hear it — as the prophet asks: "Can a shofar be blown in a city and the people not tremble?" (*Amos* 3:6).

8. The shofar reminds us of the great and awesome Judgment Day of the future — which is described as "a day of shofar blowing and shouting" (*Zephaniah* 1:16).

9. The shofar makes us yearn for the ingathering of the exiles, of which it is said: "And it will be on that day, that a great shofar will be blown, and then ... they shall prostrate themselves to Hashem on the holy mountain in Jerusalem" (*Isaiah* 27:13).

10. The shofar recalls the revivification of the dead, which will be accompanied by the sounding of a shofar, as it is said: "All inhabitants of the world and dwellers of the earth ... you shall hear when a shofar is sounded" (*Isaiah* 18:3).

One purpose of the shofar-blowing is to bring a favorable remembrance of Israel before Hashem. Rav Saadiah Gaon says that it is also to remind us of our commitment to Torah, which we received at Sinai, at which "the sound of the shofar grew continually much stronger" (*Exodus* 19:19). R' Levi Yitzchak of Berditchev adds another aspect to this with a parable.

> *A king went hunting accompanied by his retinue. Somehow, he was separated from them and could not find them. Darkness was descending, and he was hopelessly lost in the woods. After wandering for hours, he saw a light in the distance, and upon approaching, found it to be shining out from a hut of a woodsman. The king asked if he could stay until daybreak. The woodsman did not know the stranger's identity, but welcomed him and gave him food and a place to sleep.*
>
> *In the morning, the king revealed his identity and asked to be shown the way home. The woodsman escorted the king from the woods. In gratitude, the king gave the woodsman a dignified position in the palace and supplied him with a royal uniform.*
>
> *Years went by, and the former woodsman foolishly became entangled in a palace intrigue. The conspirators were all arrested and sentenced to death. When the woodsman was given a last wish, he asked to be allowed to put on his woodsman's clothing and appear before the king. When the king saw him clad in those garments, he remembered how the woodsman had helped him when he was lost, and pardoned him.*

R' Levi Yitzchak said, "The Midrash says that Hashem offered the Torah to the other nations, but they rejected it. The only nation that accepted the Torah and Hashem as its King was Israel. Therefore, we blow the shofar to remind Hashem of Sinai, and that we were the sole nation that accepted the Torah and recognized Him as King. This merit should warrant our receiving a favorable judgment."

The essential *kavannah* at hearing the shofar is knowing that we are thereby fulfilling Hashem's commandment. There are also many esoteric *kavannos* known to students of kabbalah.

> *Before Rosh Hashanah, R' Levi Yitzchak interviewed several candidates for the privilege of blowing the shofar for him. Each one related the mystic kavannos of the kabbalah that they knew. The final candidate was a simple but sincere Jew, and R' Levi Yitzchak was surprised to think that he would know kabbalistic kavannos.*
>
> *The man said, "Rebbe, I know nothing about kabbalah. My only kavannah is that I have several daughters of marriageable age, but I cannot find chassanim [bridegrooms] for them because I don't have the money for their dowries. My kavannah is, 'Master of the universe! I am going to blow the shofar to fulfill Your wish as you told us in the Torah. Please, Hashem, fulfill my wish and bless me with the means to be able to marry off my daughters.'"*
>
> *R' Levi Yitzchak was impressed by the man's sincerity. "That is the finest kavannah," he said. "You will blow the shofar for me."*

The mitzvah of shofar is very dear to the Jewish people, as is evidenced by the crowded attendance in shul, which includes mothers with tiny infants in their arms or in carriages. This led to the comment by R' Pinchos Horowitz, author of *Haflaah*, who cited the Talmud, "Why do we blow shofar on Rosh Hashanah? To confuse Satan" (*Rosh Hashanah* 16a). Rashi comments that when Satan sees how devoted the Jews are to mitzvos, he is silenced.

R' Pinchos asks, "Wouldn't the Jews' devotion to mitzvos provoke Satan to bring even more charges against them?" He answers by citing the Talmud stating that when a person does *teshuvah* out of love for Hashem, his sins are converted to merits (*Yoma* 86b). Therefore, when Satan sees the fervor and love with which the Jews observe the mitzvah of shofar, he does not want to charge them with committing sins, lest these, too, will be converted to merits.

R' Simchah Bunim of Pshische gave yet another interpretation to the above Talmudic quotation. "We say to Satan, 'If hearing the shofar so confuses you that you cannot do your mission, by what right do you bring charges against us that we are derelict in performing mitzvos? We are constantly under the pressure of trying to feed our families and dealing with the many stresses in life. These are far greater stresses than hearing the sound of a shofar. If the latter is enough to upset you, how dare you bring charges against us?' "

Bnei Yisaschar points out something remarkable. We blow the shofar with varied sounds: *tekiah* — a long simple sound; *shevarim* — a broken sound, as if a sick person is groaning in pain; and *teruah* — brief whimpering sounds, as if one is crying in grief. We then have a total of one hundred blasts of the shofar. Yet, all the Torah says about Rosh Hashanah is *Yom Teruah*, a day of shofar-blowing. How did this complex service result from that single word?

The Sages derived all the laws of shofar through exegesis, using the thirteen rules by which the Torah is expounded, compiled by R' Yishmael (Introduction to *Sifra*).

R' DovBer, the Maggid of Mezeritch, said that the thirteen rules of R' Yishmael correspond to the Thirteen Attributes of Hashem's Mercy. Hence, when we implement the thirteen rules, we invoke the Thirteen Principles of Mercy. Therefore, the complex order of blowing the shofar, which was arrived at by application of the thirteen rules of R' Yishmael, bodes well for eliciting a favorable judgment, as Hashem will relate to us according to the Thirteen Principles of Mercy.

If the first day of Rosh Hashanah falls on Shabbos, we do not blow the shofar. Why not? Because everyone is aware that it is a mitzvah to blow shofar, but not everyone is well versed in the laws of Shabbos. Someone who does not know exactly how to blow the shofar, and wishes to learn how, might carry the shofar on Shabbos. To prevent this person from carrying the shofar through a public thoroughfare in violation of Shabbos, the Sages used their authority to passively set aside the mitzvah of shofar (*Rosh Hashanah* 29b).

But let's think about this. It is difficult to meet the specifications of a public thoroughfare that would render carrying a Scriptural violation of Shabbos. Such a thoroughfare may exist only in a major metropolis. Most Jews do not live in proximity to such a thoroughfare. Furthermore, the scenario of a person carrying the shofar on Shabbos is rather unlikely. Yet, to prevent this remote possibility, the Sages saw fit to deprive *hundreds of thousands of Jews* of fulfilling a Scriptural mitzvah every time Rosh Hashanah falls on Shabbos! (The mitzvah of shofar on the second day of Rosh Hashanah is Rabbinic rather than Scriptural.) Throughout the ages, many *millions* of Jews did not fulfill the Scriptural mitzvah in order to prevent the remote possibility of a person committing an *inadvertent* sin!

HaGaon HaRav Aharon Kotler said, "If you think deeply about this, you will realize the gravity of even a single inadvertent sin, whose avoidance justified canceling a Scriptural mitzvah, leaving millions of Jews bereft of the opportunity to fulfill it."

In a lighter vein, Chassidim say that the angel assigned to carry the mitzvah of shofar to Hashem also has the assignment of keeping the *cholent* hot on Shabbos. Inasmuch as an angel cannot fulfill two assignments simultaneously, the mitzvah of shofar yields to the priority of the *cholent*.

While this is obviously related in jest, there is some validity to it. The sect of the Karaites observed the Scripture literally, and did not accept the authority of the Sages' interpretation. Inasmuch as the Torah says, "You shall not kindle fire in any of your dwellings on the Sabbath day" (*Exodus* 35:3), they sat in the dark and consumed only cold food on Shabbos. The Sages interpreted this verse to mean that we may not *kindle* a flame on Shabbos, but we may enjoy the light of a lamp that was lit before Shabbos, and we may eat food that has been kept hot as specified by halachah.

Our eating *cholent* is thus a testimony of our acceptance of the authority of the Sages, who, therefore, also had the power to interpret a Scriptural mitzvah so that it is properly observed. Hence, shofar on Shabbos is canceled so that the angel can tend to the *cholent*.

When R' Heschel of Cracow was a child, he helped himself to some goodies on Rosh Hashanah before the morning services. His father reprimanded him, "Don't you know that it is improper to eat before you hear the shofar?"

Young Heschel responded, "Yes, I know, but I have a good reason.

"Every day of Elul, we blow the shofar in the morning service. However, on the day before Rosh Hashanah, we do not blow the shofar. This is to confuse Satan, so that he should not know which day is Rosh Hashanah and will not bring charges against the Jews.

"I, too, wished to confuse Satan. He knows that we don't eat on Rosh Hashanah morning before hearing the shofar. When he sees me eating, he will think, 'Oh, today must not be Rosh Hashanah.' In this way, I will have tricked him."

The baal tokeia (person designated to blow the shofar) of R' Shlomo of Radomsk was a tzaddik and a Torah scholar. One Rosh Hashanah he was unable to get a sound out of the shofar, regardless of how much he tried. R' Shlomo then called one of the other worshipers, a young man with scant knowledge of Torah, who blew the shofar flawlessly.

The baal tokeia felt very sad. For years he had blown the shofar, and now he had failed.

R' Shlomo comforted him and told him the following story.

A recently enthroned king had a new crown designed for him, and he engaged some of the finest diamond-cutters in the country to cut the diamonds. However, they all declined, because they were afraid that even the tiniest error in cutting the jewels might be dealt with harshly. The king finally prevailed on the best craftsman in the country to cut the stones. However, just as he was about to cut the diamond that was to be used as the centerpiece of the crown, he became so anxious that his hands trembled and he could not do the work.

The king then called in an apprentice diamond-cutter, a rather dull young man who had no concept of the status of the king or the importance of the crown, and he cut the diamond properly. The expert could not do so, because he was so overwhelmed by the awesomeness of the task that he could not prevent his hands from shaking. The young apprentice did not have this fear.

"So it was with blowing the shofar," R' Shlomo said to the baal tokeia. "You were overcome with the awesomeness of the mitzvah, which caused you so much anxiety that you could not blow the shofar. This young man had no such anxiety, and that is why he could blow the shofar easily."

לַמְנַצֵּחַ לִבְנֵי קֹרַח מִזְמוֹר
For the Conductor, by the sons of Korach, a song.

The sevenfold recitation of Psalm 47 is based on the kabbalistic concept that there are fifty levels of impurity. As long as one has not descended into the lowest, the fiftieth level, there can be redemption.

The Ari *z"l* said that in Egypt, the Jews had descended to the forty-ninth level, and the reason for their great haste in leaving Egypt was because if they had descended to the fiftieth level, they would have been lost forever.

Psalm 47 contains Hashem's Name, Elokim, seven times, in reference to His dispensing strict justice. When we recite this psalm seven times, we invoke Hashem's attribute of justice forty-nine times, in order to impel us to rise from the depths of the forty-nine levels of impurity. When we have emerged from this state of impurity, we pray that Hashem will change His Attribute of Justice to His Attribute of Mercy.

R' Levi Yitzchak of Berditchev had a novel interpretation of verse 7, *zamru l'Elokim zameru*. The appellation *Elokim* refers to Hashem's conducting the world with strict justice. The word *zamru,* in addition to meaning "make music," can also mean to "cut away" (see *Leviticus* 25:4). Thus, we hope to "cut away" the attribute of strict justice so that Hashem will judge us with mercy.

הָרִיעוּ לֵאלֹקִים בְּקוֹל רִנָּה
Sound the shofar to Hashem, with a cry of joy.

R' Levi Yitzchak of Berditchev says that when the king's servants approach him to submit their petitions, they are so awed by the king's majesty that they are afraid to speak, lest their words do not come out properly, just as Moses was reluctant to go to Pharaoh because of his speech impediment. Therefore, they try to convey their needs by gesture rather than verbally.

So, too, we, awed by the majesty of Hashem, are fearful that we may trip over our words, and Satan will seize hold of our misstatements to prosecute us. Therefore, we deliver our petition via the sound of the shofar, a heartfelt cry. We rejoice in the knowledge that Hashem will receive this petition with grace, just as a father is pleased when his infant son, who cannot pronounce words, makes sounds indicating that he wishes to communicate with him.

If the shofar makes us tremble, how can we feel joy? It might seem that joy and fear cannot coexist. Obviously, they can, because the psalmist says, "Rejoice with trembling" (*Psalms* 2:11). But how can this be done?

> *A chassid of R' Shneur Zalman presented the Rebbe with a "kvittel," a petition listing all his needs for which he sought the Rebbe's blessing. The Rebbe studied the kvittel and then said, "It seems that you have given much thought to your needs. Have you also given much thought to why you are needed?"*
>
> *The chassid was shaken by the Rebbe's admonition, but was also elated by the Rebbe's statement that he was needed! The Rebbe said that he was needed in the world, that he had a mission, a purpose for being alive. That was an uplifting thought. He was both trembling and joyous.*

So it is with the shofar. It arouses us to *teshuvah*, but at the same time, it teaches us that Hashem desires our *teshuvah*.

יִבְחַר לָנוּ אֶת נַחֲלָתֵנוּ, אֶת גְּאוֹן יַעֲקֹב אֲשֶׁר אָהֵב

**He will choose our heritage for us, the pride
of Jacob that He loves .....**

Alshich says that the word "heritage" refers to the Third Temple. The Talmud says, "[The Temple] is not like Abraham, who called [Moriah] 'mountain' [*Genesis* 22:14]; and not like Isaac, who referred to it as 'field' (ibid. 24:63); but like Jacob, who referred to it as 'abode' (ibid. 28:17)." The first Temple was built in Abraham's merit, and the Second Temple was built in Isaac's merit. These edifices did not endure. The Third Temple, which will be in Jacob's merit, will be eternal. This is what the psalmist refers to as the "pride of Jacob."

Rav Gershon Meir Biersky explained this verse with a parable.

*A well-to-do man, an accomplished Torah scholar,
sought a learned young man as a husband for his
daughter. He went to the yeshivah and announced that
the student who could resolve a very difficult problem
in the Talmud would receive his daughter's hand in
marriage. Of course, everyone aspired to become this
affluent man's son-in-law.*

*The wealthy man presented the problem in the
Talmud. Several students suggested possible resolutions,
but none were satisfactory. His efforts having proven
unsuccessful, he left the yeshivah.*

After his coach began moving, he heard someone shouting, "Please stop! Please stop!" He saw that a student was running after him. The student said, "I don't know how to resolve the problem, so I cannot marry your daughter. But please, tell me the resolution to the problem. It is Torah, and I want to understand it."

The man welcomed the student into the coach, and gave him the correct resolution to the problem. The student thanked him and stood up to leave the carriage. The man stopped him, saying, "Don't leave. I want you as my son-in-law. Let us go back and tell the Rosh Yeshivah that we have a mazal tov."

When they returned to the yeshivah, some of the students asked the wealthy man, "Why did you choose him? In what way is he better than we are?"

The man answered, "You were all motivated by the desire to marry my daughter. He was the only one whose primary interest is to understand the Torah."

R' Gershon Meir continued, "We all want the Redemption, but for what reason? To be free of the oppression that we suffer in exile. The true reason for wanting the Redemption is that Hashem will do away with the *yetzer hara* and remove all the barriers between Him and us.

"He will choose our heritage for us, the pride of Jacob that *He* loves." That is, the pride that Hashem loves is the spiritual wealth that we will achieve, not the physical comforts that we desire.

עָלָה אֱלֹקִים בִּתְרוּעָה, ה' בְּקוֹל שׁוֹפָר

God has ascended with a blast; Hashem,
with the sound of the shofar.

On Rosh Hashanah Hashem "ascends" from the Throne of Judgment to the Throne of Mercy.

R' Shlomo of Lentshne cites the verse in which the word *teru'as* means "friendship of" (*Numbers* 23:21). He applies that translation here: God has ascended to the Throne of Mercy with *teruah*, meaning that when Jews are united in friendship, Hashem conducts Himself to them with mercy rather than with harsh judgment, as the Midrash says, "Shalom is so great that even if the Jews were to worship idols, if they are united as one, the harsh judgments cannot touch them" (*Tanchuma Tzav* 7).

זַמְּרוּ אֱלֹהִים זַמֵּרוּ, זַמְּרוּ לְמַלְכֵּנוּ

Make music for God, make music, make music for our King

Rabbi Samson Raphael Hirsch notes that some chapters in *Psalms* are entitled *mizmor*, while others are called *shir*. R' Hirsch says that these represent two different concepts. *Mizmor* is related to the concept of "to prune" or "to cut away." *Shir*, on the other hand, in Talmud means "a leash," and the connotation is "connection" or "drawing closer." There are times when the primary effort is *mizmor*, to cut away the obstacles that interfere with our relationship to Hashem. At other times, the effort is *shir*, to draw closer to Hashem.

A similar thought is expressed by R' Levi Yitzchak of Berditchev. The word for "make music" is *zamru*, which is followed by *L'Elokim*, the name used for Hashem when He conducts the world using *din* (strict judgment). The verse can thus be read as "Cut through the *middah* of *din*," and appeal to Hashem to relate to us with *rachamim* (compassion).

☞ Prefatory Verses

מִן הַמֵּצַר
From the straits ....

"From the straits did I call upon God. He responded by giving me expansiveness" (*Psalms* 118:5).

A person who experiences severe suffering prays only for relief from his distress. At that point he does not ask for the extras he would ask for when he is well. King David says, "Not only did Hashem deliver me from my suffering, but He also expanded His mercy and gave me many blessings for which I had not asked."

This verse is symbolized by the shofar, which is very narrow at one end and broad at the other. Similarly, one may feel oppressed by constraints, but Hashem provides relief with expansiveness.

David is referring to his own distress, when he fled from King Saul, taking refuge in caves, but thereafter he became king. David also intended this prophetically, referring to times when Jews would suffer in exile, but Hashem will return them to their greatness.

קוֹלִי שָׁמָעְתָּ, אַל תַּעְלֵם אָזְנְךָ לְרַוְחָתִי לְשַׁוְעָתִי
You have heard my voice; do not shut Your ear from my prayer for my relief, when I cry out (Lamentations 3:56).

In the Chabad *machzor,* this verse is replaced with "Hear my voice in accordance with Your kindness; O Hashem, preserve me in accordance with Your practice ..." (*Psalms* 119:149). R' Shneur Zalman, the Baal HaTanya, pointed out that the remaining five verses, whose first letters along with the first letter of the first verse, form the acronym *kera Satan* (destroy Satan), are all taken from Psalm 119. Why would the Sages have inserted this single verse from *Lamentations*? He reasons, therefore, that the Sages actually intended verse 149 in Psalm 119. The first words of this verse and the verse in *Lamentations* are almost identical, and it seems that the person who compiled the first *machzor* mistakenly assumed that the verse from *Lamentations* was intended.

R' Shneur Zalman's logic is interesting. Nevertheless, there are grounds to assume that if *Klal Yisrael* adopts a practice, it is valid even if its source was an error. Therefore, we say the verse from *Lamentations* as it is found in our *machzor*.

רֹאשׁ דְּבָרְךָ אֱמֶת, וּלְעוֹלָם כָּל מִשְׁפַּט צִדְקֶךָ

Your very first utterance is truth, and Your righteous judgment is eternal (Psalms 119:160).

In the account of Creation, the Torah begins with. "בְּרֵאשִׁית בָּרָא אֱלֹקִים— In the beginning of God's creating" (*Genesis* 1:1). The last letters of the first three Hebrew words can be arranged to spell *emes* — truth. The last letters of the final three words in the account of Creation are "אֲשֶׁר בָּרָא אֱלֹקִים לַעֲשׂוֹת — which God created to make" (ibid. 2:3). These Hebrew letters also spell *emes*. This is to indicate that the foundation of the world is *emes*.

The *sefarim* (Torah writings) point out that the three letters of the word *emes* are the first, middle, and last letters of the alphabet, indicating that truth has a stable footing, and as such is eternal. This is conveyed by our verse, "Your very first utterance [the beginning of Creation] is truth, and Your righteous judgment is eternal."

The Talmud comments that when the nations of the world heard Hashem say, "I am the Lord, your God," they believed that He was asking for His personal glory. When Hashem said, "Honor your father and mother," the nations realized their error and admitted that Hashem was not seeking personal glory (*Kiddushin* 31a).

This verse should remind us that nothing is written in the Torah because Hashem needs it. Hashem is All-perfect. "If you were righteous, what have you given Him, or what has He taken from your hand?" (*Job* 35:7). "The mitzvos were given to Israel for no purpose other than to refine them [the people]" (*Vayikra Rabbah* 13:3). We must understand that all the mitzvos in the Torah are for our benefit, not for Hashem's benefit.

עֲרוֹב עַבְדְּךָ לְטוֹב, אַל יַעַשְׁקֻנִי זֵדִים

Be Your servant's guarantor for good, let not willful sinners exploit me (Psalms 119:122).

The apparent meaning of this verse is that David is asking for Hashem to protect him from his enemies.

A Chassidic interpretation is based on the verse, "Turn from evil and do good" (ibid. 34:15); one must cleanse himself of sins, lest the forces of evil interfere with his mitzvah observance. Before beginning his Torah study, the Seer of Lublin would say, "Forgive my sins, Hashem, so that I should not be like those of whom it is said, 'But to the wicked, God said, "To what purpose do you recount My decrees and bear My covenant upon your lips?"'" (ibid. 50:16).

The above verse can thus be read as "Protect me when I do good [perform mitzvos], so that the forces of evil do not rob me of them."

A novel interpretation is given by Radak, who notes that the word *arov* (guarantor) may be translated as "pleasing, sweet," as in *Malachi* 3:4. The verse then reads "May Your servant be pleasing to You."

שָׂשׂ אָנֹכִי עַל אִמְרָתֶךָ, כְּמוֹצֵא שָׁלָל רָב.
I rejoice over Your word, like one who finds
abundant spoils (Psalms 119:162).

This verse requires a bit of explanation. A person who finds abundant spoils has not made any effort in their acquisition, whereas acquiring Torah requires effort: "If someone says, 'I exerted myself and acquired Torah,' you should believe him. If one says, 'I acquired Torah without exerting myself,' do not believe him" (*Megillah* 6b). It would appear that acquisition of Torah cannot be compared to finding abundant spoils.

Yet there is truth in this. The psalmist refers to Moses' receiving the Torah by stating, "You ascended on high and took captive [referring to wresting the Torah from the angels], you took gifts for man." The commentaries note that the Hebrew word for "you took" connotes "purchase," in which the buyer pays for an item, yet the verse refers to Torah as a "gift." They answer that both aspects are true. The Talmud says that Moses learned and forgot, learned and forgot, until Hashem gave him the Torah as a gift (*Nedarim* 38a). Thus, it was both a "purchase," in that he invested considerable effort to obtain Torah, and because he made such great effort, Hashem rewarded him with Torah as a gift.

David devoted much effort in study of the Torah. Psalm 119 is replete with references to his exerting himself in Torah study, but he also says, "Unveil my eyes so that I may see the wonders of Your Torah"; i.e., Hashem should enable him to see the secrets of Torah that are inaccessible solely through one's effort.

"I rejoice over Your word like one who finds abundant spoils" — thus David expresses his joy at the gift Hashem has given him, the vast knowledge of Torah that he received beyond his efforts.

> *The Maggid of Mezeritch related a parable of a person who was wandering in the wilderness and came across an enormous pile of gold coins. He quickly filled all his pockets with the coins, but this was but a small fraction of the total, and a huge heap remained. He walked away, joyous over the wealth he had found but sad because there was so much more he could have taken had he had a wagon. He vowed to return for more gold if he could find his way back.*
>
> *So it is with Torah. We rejoice over what we have taken from Torah, but Torah is infinite, and there is so much more that we are leaving behind. But we are always able to go back for more. We know the way, and we have the means.*

טוֹב טַעַם וָדַעַת לַמְּדֵנִי, כִּי בְמִצְוֺתֶיךָ הֶאֱמָנְתִּי

Teach me good reasoning and knowledge,
for I believe in Your commandments (Psalms 119:66).

The Talmud says that Hashem did not reveal the rationale

for the mitzvos, because a person might think that if a particular reason does not apply to him, he is not obligated to observe that mitzvah (*Sanhedrin* 20b). The Talmud gives an example of a mitzvah whose reason was revealed: the king "shall not take many wives, so that his heart should not turn astray" (*Deuteronomy* 17:17). King Solomon felt secure in himself, confident that he would not be led away from Torah; hence he felt that this restriction did not apply to him. He did take many wives, and they did have a negative effect on him.

The danger is that one may observe the mitzvos only because he thinks he understands their purpose. If one firmly believes in the mitzvos and observes them even though he does not understand their purpose, then he may seek such understanding.

This is what the psalmist says, "Teach me good reasoning and knowledge"; i.e., help me understand the reasons for the mitzvos, because "I believe in Your commandments"; i.e., I observe them whether or not I understand their purpose, and I am not at risk of deviating from the true path because of such knowledge (*Imros Tehoros*).

נִדְבוֹת פִּי רְצֵה נָא, ה׳, וּמִשְׁפָּטֶיךָ לַמְּדֵנִי
Please accept with favor the offerings of my mouth,
Hashem, and teach me Your judgments (Psalms 119:108).

The word *nidvos* refers to voluntary offerings, donations above and beyond what is required of a person. The halachic requirements of speech are to avoid *lashon hara*, falsehood, carrying tales, and indecent language. *Tzaddikim* were extremely cautious to guard their speech, so as not to utter a word other than in the service of Hashem. When a person prays, he indeed says the right words, but if his mind wanders and he has scant *kavannah* in his prayers, they are inadequate. Indeed, Rambam rules that if a person did not have proper *kavannah* in the first *berachah* of the *Amidah*, it is as if he did not say it, and he must repeat it (*Laws of Tefillah* 4:15). Nevertheless, today we do not repeat the *Amidah* even if we *davened* without proper *kavannah*, because the second recitation will doubtless also be said without the proper *kavannah*.

The Talmud relates that R' Chanina ben Dosa said, "When I pray for someone's health, I can tell from the nature of my prayer whether the person I pray for will live or not. If my prayer flows smoothly, then I know that it was accepted."

Imros Tehoros explains that R' Chanina never spoke an idle word. Hence, if Hashem were not going to answer his prayer, Hashem would not allow him to say the words of prayer, so that they not turn out to be said in vain. In this way, R' Chanina knew whether or not his prayer was effective.

This is what David said, "Please accept with favor the offerings of my mouth, Hashem, and teach me Your judgments." David's speech was always holy, equivalent to offerings. Thereby, like R' Chanina, David could know Hashem's judgments and whether his prayer was effective.

בָּרוּךְ אַתָּה ... וְצִוָּנוּ לִשְׁמוֹעַ קוֹל שׁוֹפָר
Blessed are You ... and commanded us to hearken
to the sound of the shofar.

It is noteworthy that the *berachah* is not "to blow the shofar" but rather "to hearken to the sound of the shofar." The Hebrew *lishmoa*, "to listen" or "to hearken," also means "to understand."

> *A maggid once preached a sermon, but the people were not moved by it. Someone said to him, "Your words must not have come from your heart, because the Talmud says that words that come from the heart enter the heart."*
>
> *The maggid replied, "A blacksmith had an assistant who would blow on the fire to increase the flame. One day, he visited a blacksmith in the city and saw that he was using a bellows. He was thrilled by his discovery and bought a bellows.*
>
> *"When he returned home, he tried to use the bellows, but without success. He reported his failure to the city blacksmith, who said, 'Are you sure you had a spark?' When he said that he did not, the blacksmith said, 'The bellows makes a large flame only if there is a spark. Without a spark, the bellows does nothing.'"*
>
> *The maggid continued, "Words from the heart enter the heart only if there is a spark of teshuvah in the heart. Without that spark in your hearts, my words can do nothing."*

The mitzvah is not to blow the shofar, but rather to hear the sound of the shofar. In fact, if one blows the shofar in a deep pit where he hears the echo of the sound rather than the sound of the shofar itself, he has not fulfilled the mitzvah. We must hearken to the sound of the shofar to awaken feelings of repentance, but if we do not have a spark of *teshuvah* that the shofar can arouse, hearing it accomplishes nothing.

אַשְׁרֵי הָעָם יוֹדְעֵי תְרוּעָה ...

Praises to the people who know the shofar's cry;
Hashem, by the illumination of Your countenance they walk.
In Your Name they rejoice all day long, and through Your
righteousness they are exalted. For You are the splendor of
their power, and through Your favor our pride will be exalted
(Psalms 89:16-18).

The Midrash asks, "Is Israel the only people who know how to blow the shofar? Why, all the nations have musicians who play musical instruments! What the psalmist means is, 'Praises to the people who know how to appease their Creator with the shofar blast'" (*Vayikra Rabbah* 29). In what way do we know how to appease Hashem with the shofar?

It is said of the great *tzaddikim* that their only desire was to be in the glow of the *Shechinah* (Divine Presence), as David said, "One thing I asked of Hashem, that shall I seek: Would that I dwell in the House of Hashem all the days of my life, to behold the sweetness of Hashem and to contemplate in His Sanctuary" (*Psalms* 27:4).

This is the theme of the Rosh Hashanah prayers: the world will come to acknowledge the sovereignty of Hashem, as we say in the *Amidah*, "And so, too, Hashem, our God, instill Your awe upon all Your works"; "Then You, Hashem, will reign alone over all Your works"; "Our God and God of our forefathers, reign over the entire universe in Your glory."

What is true of the *tzaddikim* is true of *Klal Yisrael*. Throughout our history we have experienced devastating suffering — expulsions, crusades, pogroms, Holocaust — but we stubbornly cling to our faith in Hashem and to the promise of Redemption. Our hope is eternal that we shall one day walk in the light of Hashem, when His sovereignty is universally acclaimed.

We sound the shofar with the *shevarim* — the broken sounds of a sick person groaning in pain — and *teruah* — the brief whimpering sounds of one crying in grief — to express the suffering of *Klal Yisrael* throughout the ages. Yet, "In Your Name they rejoice all day long, and through Your righteousness they are exalted. For You are the splendor of their power, and through Your favor our pride will be exalted." This is our wisdom, the source of our knowledge of how to appease our Creator with the shofar blast.

Mussaf

Chazzan's Prayer

*T*he Mussaf service is preceded by the *chazzan* chanting the prayer *Hineni he'ani mimaas* (Here I am, impoverished of deeds), in which he declares himself unworthy to be the congregation's agent, leading them in prayer to Hashem.

Ironically, the *chazzan's* self-effacement is the very thing that makes him worthy of this role. Hashem said, "I abide in exaltedness and holiness — but I am with the despondent and lowly of spirit" (*Isaiah* 57:15).

The *chazzan* asks Hashem to "denounce the Satan, that he not impede me." The *chazzan's* self-effacement may also be effective in thwarting the Satan, according to a parable told by the *Shelah* (R' Yeshayah HaLevi Horowitz, 1558-1628).

> *One of the king's ministers evoked the envy of other government officials, and they plotted to have him accused of treason. He was imprisoned, and the conspirators knew that if he were to send a message to the king, he would be able to exonerate himself. Therefore, they cautioned the prison guards to make sure that he did not have the opportunity to send any messages.*

> *One day, the minister saw the trash collector*
> *gathering all the refuse in the prison. He reasoned*
> *that no one would think that he would make the trash*
> *collector his messenger to the king, so that is precisely*
> *what he did, and he succeeded in having his message*
> *relayed to the king.*

Satan is on the alert to prevent our prayers from reaching Hashem. As the *chazzan* declares himself sinful and unworthy, Satan is thrown off-guard, assuming that this person would certainly not be the one chosen to bring the people's prayers to Hashem. The Satan therefore pays no attention to the *chazzan*, who then succeeds in conveying the congregation's prayers to Hashem.

☞ *Malchios, Zichronos, Shofros*
(Kingship, Remembrance, Shofar)

The core of the Mussaf service is *Malchios, Zichronos, Shofros*. This is based on the Talmudic statement, "Hashem said, Recite *Malchios* before Me, that you may accept My sovereignty over you. Recite *Zichronos* before Me, that your remembrances will come before Me, and this will be achieved with the shofar" (*Rosh Hashanah* 34b). During the *Amidah*, we recite ten verses on each theme, culled from the *Chumash*, the Prophets, and the Writings.

One might ask, do we not accept Hashem's sovereignty multiple times every day? When we recite a *berachah*, we refer to Hashem as *Melech HaOlam*, King of the universe.

True, but the psychology of the human mind requires that some things must be called to our attention. On Rosh Hashanah we concentrate specifically on Hashem's sovereignty, and we pray for the day that all the nations in the entire world will accept Hashem as their King.

☞ *Malchios*

> ### *Hashem said, "Recite Malchios before Me, that you may accept My sovereignty over you.'*

Malchios refers to *kabbalas ol malchus Shamayim*, acceptance of the "yoke" of Hashem's rule. The term "yoke" is used to indicate that we observe the mitzvos not because we think they are reasonable, but because they are Hashem's commandments and we must fulfill them whether or not we understand the reasoning behind them.

> *A father was reciting the Haggadah, saying, "Avadim hayinu, we were slaves to Pharaoh in Egypt, and Hashem delivered us from enslavement." His young son asked, "But Abba, you told me that we are avadim, slaves to Hashem. So we just traded one kind of enslavement for another."*
>
> *The father responded, "But we accept our being avadim to Hashem every day when we say Shema. We gladly and willingly submit to Hashem's rule. A person has bechirah [free choice] and conceivably may decide not to accept Hashem's rule, chas v'shalom. When we were slaves to Pharaoh we did not have the freedom to choose whether we wanted to be slaves to him. We are benei chorin, free people, and we freely accept Hashem's rule over us.*

— 151 —

The concept of *ol malchus Shamayim* as a yoke might cause one to think that observance of Torah is a burden. Nothing could be further from the truth. The "yoke" of Hashem's commandments is not incompatible with joy, as King David says, "Serve Hashem with awe, that you may rejoice when there is trembling" (*Psalms* 2:11). Indeed, on Shabbos we say, *"yismechu bemalchuscha,"* we rejoice in being subjects to the King, Hashem.

> *An emissary from Eretz Yisrael came to Europe to raise funds for the yishuv, the Jews in the Holy Land, who were impoverished. Emissaries from Eretz Yisrael were highly esteemed, and he feared that accepting honor because he came from the Holy Land was exploiting the Land for personal gain. He actually prayed that if he was honored, he would feel pain, to distract him from the honor he received.*
>
> *He came to R' Mordechai of Lechovitch, who received him with great honor, He developed such severe pain that he could not sit at the tzaddik's Shabbos table and found it necessary to lie down. When he heard the tzaddik and the Chassidim singing "yismechu bemalchuscha," he jumped up, not even pausing to don his shoes and coat, and ran into the room, dancing around the table, and declaring, "We rejoice in nothing else, not even in our families, not in our possessions, but only in Your kingdom."*

It would be truly wonderful if we achieved *kabalas ol malchus Shamayim* by reciting the ten verses of *Malchios*.

*A chassid prevailed upon the gabbai (sexton) of the
Tzaddik of Sanz to allow him to be present when the
Tzaddik awoke. He heard the Tzaddik begin to recite,
"Modeh ani," saying, "Modeh ani lefanecha Melech …."
Then he paused, repeated, "… Melech …" and paused
again. "I don't feel 'Melech' yet," he cried out. After
meditating a while, and repeatedly saying, "Melech," he
went on to say, "chai vekayam."*

The Maggid of Trisk cited the Talmud (*Berachos* 58a) that
states, "The kingdom of Heaven operates similarly to the earthly
kingdom" (*Berachos* 58a). The Maggid explained, "It is customary,
when a new king is crowned, that he gives amnesty to all offenders.
When we enthrone Hashem on Rosh Hashanah, it is like a coronation, and He will grant amnesty to the sinful."

*Meir Nesivos describes the coronation of the Russian
czar. Preparations began one month prior to the event.
The streets were cleaned and festooned. Tickets to the
coronation were at a premium. One who was able to get
a ticket considered himself to be the luckiest person in the
world.*

*Soldiers and police were dressed in spotless uniforms
with gleaming buttons. People with tickets were clad in
their finery and arrived at the palace hours before the
coronation ceremony was to begin.*

*During the ceremony, the ministers lined up on the
platform. A decorated soldier withdrew the crown from
its case and handed it to the lowest-ranking minister, who
handed it to the next in rank, and so on until it reached*

the prime minister, who placed the crown on the head of the czar. Imagine the emotion and the pride of the prime minister when he put the crown on the head of the czar!

If this is so with an earthly king, how much more so with the King of kings! Not only are we accorded a personal invitation to the coronation, but Hashem says to us individually, "Recite *Malchios* before Me, that you may accept My sovereignty over you." We each have the honor of *veyitnu lecha kesser meluchah*, placing the crown on Hashem, so to speak. If we only realized what it is that we are doing, how euphoric we would be!

As was noted, the theme of Rosh Hashanah is "Kingship." The selected verses from Scripture are on this theme, as are the *piyutim,* i.e., *Melech Elyon* (Supreme King).

☞ *Aleinu — It Is Our Duty*

The introduction to *Malchios* is *Aleinu,* a prayer familiar to us because we recite it at the close of each daily Shacharis, Minchah, and Maariv service.

> *A folk tale relates that the Aleinu prayer came before Hashem with a complaint. "I am treated very shabbily," it said. "Some people hurry out of shul at the end of davening and pay no attention to me. Others recite my words while they are putting away their talleisim. I do not get the respect that other prayers do."*
>
> *Hashem said to Aleinu, "As compensation, I will put you in the midst of the tefillah on Rosh Hashanah and Yom Kippur. They will open the Aron Kodesh for you, and fall on their knees for you."*

We should realize that the *kedushah* of *Aleinu* is very great, and treat it with great respect every day.

Aleinu cites our uniqueness in acknowledging Hashem as God, whereas other peoples may pray to worthless idols.

> *A Jew suffered the heartbreak of seeing his house burn down. Neighbors saw him dancing in front of the flaming house, singing, "Shelo asani goy" (that He did not make me a non-Jew). They thought that the tragedy of seeing his house in flames had caused him to become insane, but he explained, "When the house of a non-Jew burns down, the idols he worships are consumed in the fire. Although I lost my house, my God is intact."*

וְיָדַעְתָּ הַיּוֹם וַהֲשֵׁבֹתָ אֶל לְבָבֶךָ ...

***You are to know this day and take to your heart that
Hashem is the only God — in Heaven above and on
the earth below — there is none other.***

The apparent meaning of the phrase, "there is none other," is that there is no god other than Hashem. One of the commentaries added an interpretation, "You are to know this day etc. ... *there is nothing else you need to know.*"

The Talmud states that Moses gave us the 613 mitzvos. David condensed them to eleven principles, Isaiah to six principles, and Micah to three principles. The prophet Habakkuk condensed them to a single principle: The righteous person shall live through his *emunah* (faith) (*Habbakuk* 2:4). Obviously, none of these prophets discarded any of the 613 mitzvos. Rather, they provided all-encompassing principles that contain all of Torah. Habakkuk's statement is that if a person has true *emunah*, it will lead him to observe all of Torah.

That is the meaning of the above interpretation of "there is none other — *there is nothing else you need to know.*" This knowledge will enable one to reach everything else he needs to know.

☞ *Achan and Mutual Responsibility*

The tradition (*Seder HaYom*) is that the paragraph after *Aleinu*, *Al kein nekaveh* (Therefore we put our hope), was composed by Achan. In the conquest of Canaan, the Jews triumphed over the city of Jericho, and Joshua forbade the soldiers from taking any of the spoils of the city, which had been consecrated for the treasury of Hashem (*Joshua* 6:18). In the battle for the city of Ai, the Jews suffered casualties, and Hashem told Joshua that this happened because someone had taken loot from the spoils of Jericho.

Lots were cast to identify the violator, and Achan was found to have confiscated several items from the spoils (ibid. 7:1-26). Achan confessed, and was sentenced to death. Before he was executed, he composed the *Al kein nekaveh* prayer. His name is in the acronym, the first letters of the first three Hebrew words, *Al kein nekaveh* — Achan.

The episode of Achan delivers a powerful message. When Joshua asked Hashem why the Jews had suffered defeat at Ai, Hashem said, "Israel has sinned!" Only one person, Achan, had sinned, but Hashem said, "Israel has sinned." This teaches us the principle of *aravus* (mutual responsibility).

The Mishnah relates that although Achan had to be executed

because his sin had resulted in the death of thirty-six soldiers, Joshua told him that since he had confessed, he would enter Gan Eden (*Sanhedrin* 43b). *Al kein nekaveh* is the expression of a *baal teshuvah*, acknowledging the judgment of Hashem and expressing the hope and belief that the entire world will one day recognize Hashem as the true God.

The first verse delineating *Malchios* is:

> ***Hashem shall reign for all eternity (Exodus 15:18).***

This verse was declared by the Israelites after the Splitting of the Reed Sea saved them from the pursuing Egyptian army. The reason for the future tense is because all the nations of the world did not witness the miracle. With the Ultimate Redemption, all the world will acknowledge Hashem as the true God.

The second verse in *Malchios* is:

> ***He [Hashem] perceived no iniquity in Jacob, and saw no perversity in Israel; Hashem his God is with him, and the friendship of the King is in him (Numbers 23:21).***

Rashi cites the Midrash that even when Israel sins, Hashem chooses not to scrutinize their sins to the full extent of their shortcomings.

Chassidic commentaries interpret the pronoun "He" not as referring to Hashem, but to a person, and the verse then reads, "If *a person* sees no faults in others, and always judges them favorably, then he is indeed a friend of Hashem."

> *Tzaddikim were always seeking ways to exonerate Israel.*

The outstanding champion of this commendable trait
was R' Levi Yitzchak of Berditchev, who once came upon
a man who was eating on the fast of Tishah B'Av.

R' Levi Yitzchak said, "You surely must not be
aware that today is Tishah B'Av."

The man said, "No, I am aware of it."

"Ah," R' Levi Yitzchak said, "You must be under
doctor's orders not to fast."

The man said, "No, I am perfectly healthy."

R' Levi Yitzchak lifted his eyes toward heaven.
"Master of the universe," he said, "I provided two ways
for this person to defend his eating on Tishah B'Av, but
he rejected them because he insists on being truthful. See
how wonderful Your children are."

The Baal Shem Tov looked askance at *maggidim* (preachers) who chastised the people for not studying Torah adequately and for being derelict in mitzvos.

When a maggid was particularly harsh in his delivery,
the Baal Shem Tov said, "Master of the universe! Pay no
attention to him. Your children are devoted to You. This
maggid goes around preaching to raise money so that he
can marry off his children. Bless him to have money so
that he should not have to be critical of Your children."

The third verse in *Malchios* is:

And He became King in Jeshurun, when the
leaders of the people assembled, the tribes of Israel
in unity (Deuteronomy 33:5).

The verse that immediately precedes this is, "The Torah that Moses commanded us is the heritage of the Congregation of Jacob" (*Deuteronomy* 33:4). R' Yehoshua Leib Diskin interprets the verse cited in *Malchios* as telling us that the Torah is eternal to us, regardless of the society in which we dwell, and is never abrogated. The head of state may be a king presiding over a monarchy; the state may be a republic, when the leaders of the people meet to choose a supreme ruler; and the country may be a democracy, in which the ruler is chosen directly by the populace. The above verse addresses all three. Whatever the law of the land may be, Israel abides by its heritage, the Torah.

... the tribes of Israel in unity.

The Baal Shem Tov was davening the Amidah, but this time his prayer was exceedingly prolonged. His disciples waited patiently for him to finish, but when he continued, they began to drift away, one after another. The Baal Shem Tov finished the Amidah, then reassembled his disciples, and said to them:

"The king of a country was told that there is a bird that is unbelievably beautiful, and it nests in the highest branch of a tall tree. He went to see it, and wanted the bird brought to his palace. He had his soldiers form a human ladder, so that someone could reach the bird. However, some of the soldiers who formed the ladder shifted position and as a result, no one could reach the bird.

"When you were all here, I could stand on your

— 159 —

shoulders to reach the highest levels of heaven. When you left, I was no longer able to do so."

The Talmud ascribes much importance to *tefillah b'tzibbur,* communal prayer. When we *daven* together, we stand on each others' shoulders, and our prayer can reach great heights.

On the verse, "And He became King in Jeshurun, when the leaders of the people assembled, the tribes of Israel together," Rashi cites the *Sifri,* "Only when they (Israel) are united is Hashem their King, not when there is strife among them." As we shall see in the next verse, Hashem can have the status of a ruler, but not a king. Hashem relates to us as a King only when we are united.

"The tribes of Israel together." The emphasis is on "the tribes." Each tribe was unique. Israel was not meant to be a homogenous nation, but rather a heterogeneous nation in which there was unity in spite of differences, a goal which we should now pursue.

Someone asked the Baal Shem Tov, "How can the Torah demand that we love Hashem? We cannot see Him nor touch Him. How can we develop love for an abstract being?"

The Baal Shem Tov answered, "People are not abstract. Develop love for your fellow Jew, and the love for Hashem will follow."

For Hashem to be our King rather than just a ruler, we must develop a love relationship to Him. Thus, when we love one another and are united, His relationship to us is that of a King. "Hashem said, Recite *Malchios* before Me, that you may accept My sovereignty over you." Hashem wishes to relate to us as King.

The fourth verse in *Malchios* is:

> **For the kingship belongs to Hashem,**
> **and He rules the nations (Psalms 22:29).**

Two terms for "ruler" are found in this verse, *melech* and *moshel*. *Melech* refers to a king whose rule the people accept willingly, while *moshel* refers to someone who rules by force. The psalmist says that for Israel, Hashem is a *Melech*, because we willingly subjugate ourselves to His rule when we accept *ol malchus Shamayim*. However, for the nations who do not subjugate themselves to Him, Hashem is a *Moshel*.

As we say numerous times in the *Amidah*, with the Ultimate Redemption, Hashem will be universally acknowledged. This will be again expressed in the verses from the prophets.

The fifth verse in *Malchios* is:

> **And it is said: Hashem has reigned, He has donned**
> **grandeur; He has donned strength and girded**
> **Himself; even the world of men is firm,**
> **it shall not falter (Psalms 93:1).**

There seems to be a bit of a conflict here. We are told to emulate Hashem's *middos,* one of which is glory. However we are told to be exceedingly humble (*Ethics of the Fathers* 4:4), and if we have self-glorification, we will commit the sin of *ga'avah* (vanity), which is an abomination.

> *Before the Baal Shem Tov's death, his disciples asked*
> *him to whom they should look as their leader. The Baal*

Shem Tov said, "Whoever can tell you how to break your ga'avah can be your leader."

After the Baal Shem Tov's death, the disciples posed the question to the Maggid of Mezeritch, "How can one overcome ga'avah?"

The Maggid answered, "You never overcome ga'avah. This is a struggle you must continue all your life."

The Baal Shem Tov cited the Talmud, "Wherever you find the greatness of the Holy One, Blessed is He, there you find His humility" (*Megillah* 31a). Humility is the finest of all traits, and Hashem employs this trait to teach it to us. "He will have donned grandeur"; Hashem dons grandeur as if it were an external garment. His awesome majesty is intended to instill in us the fear and reverence that will deter us from transgressing His commandments.

Hashem has the ability to possess both grandeur and humility simultaneously. We mortals lack that ability. If we allow ourselves to feel glory, we may be trapped in an attitude from which we cannot escape. Therefore, we must abide by the teaching of the Talmud, to be exceedingly humble.

The sixth verse in *Malchios* is:

And it is said: Raise up your heads, O gates, and be uplifted, you everlasting entrances, so that the King of Glory may enter. Who is this King of Glory? — Hashem, the mighty and the strong, Hashem, the strong in battle. Raise up your heads, O gates, and raise up, you everlasting entrances, so that the King of Glory may enter. Who is He, this King of

— 162 —

Glory? Hashem, Master of Legions, He is the
King of Glory, Selah (Psalms 24:7-10).

The gates refer to the gates of the Temple, and the concept expressed is that Hashem has entered the Temple.

The Talmud says that when the Temple was destroyed, the prophet Jeremiah did not refer to Hashem as "awesome." "If strangers are dancing in His Sanctuary, where is His awesomeness?" Daniel did not refer to Hashem as "mighty." "If strangers enslave His children, where is His might?" The Men of the Great Assembly said, "That is precisely His awe and might, that He restrains His enormous might and allows the wicked to succeed, and His awe is evident in that one small nation can survive surrounded by so many enemies" (*Yoma* 69b).

Referring to the destruction of the First Temple, the psalmist poses the question of the prophets, "Who is this King of Glory? Where is His might and awesomeness?" And he answers, "That is precisely His awe and might." He then refers to Hashem's Presence in the Second Temple, and repeats his question upon its destruction, "Who is this King of Glory?" and answers, "Hashem, Master of Legions, He is the King of Glory, Selah." With the Ultimate Redemption and the Third Temple, the glory of Hashem will be evident to all (*Eretz HaChaim*).

The Midrash relates that when King Solomon completed the building of the Temple and sought to bring in the Ark of the Testimony, the doors would not open. He prayed fervently, reciting the verse, "Raise up your heads, O gates, and be uplifted, you everlasting entrances, so that the King of Glory may enter." Assuming that he was referring to himself as the King of Glory, the doors refused to open. Solomon then said, "Who is this King of Glory? — Hashem, the mighty and the strong, Hashem the strong in battle." Even then the doors refused to open, and Solomon pleaded, "Remember the merits of my father, David," and the door swung open. This was proof to David's adversaries that Hashem had forgiven David for the Bath-sheba incident.

R' Chaim Friedlander says that these four verses apply to two eras. The first two verses refer to the way the world is now: Hashem is strong in battle, because He assists people who are doing battle with the *yetzer hara*. The latter two verses refer to the Ultimate Redemption, when Hashem will have removed all evil from the world.

The seventh verse in *Malchios* is:

> **So said Hashem, King of Israel and its Redeemer;**
> **Hashem of Legions: I am the first and I am the last,**
> **and aside from Me there is no god (Isaiah 44:6).**

Some concepts may be a bit difficult to grasp. For example, light travels at 186,000 miles/second. In a year, light travels 5,850,000,000,000 miles. It takes a stretch of the imagination to think about such huge distances. A million light-years and 5.8 trillion miles are terms that are almost meaningless to the average person. Yet, we can try to envision such numbers.

However, "infinity" and "eternity" are totally meaningless to us. We have never experienced anything that is without beginning and without end. Our minds are simply not geared to deal with such concepts, and if we try to do so, all sorts of distortions may result. This is why the Talmud says, "Don't seek to understand that which is beyond your ability. Think about things that are permitted. You have no business delving into the hidden things" (*Chagigah* 13a).

The opening words of the Ten Commandments are, "I am the Lord your God Who has taken you out of the land of Egypt" (*Exodus* 20:2). *Kuzari* says that Hashem did not say "I am the Lord your God Who created the world," because there had been no one to witness that assertion. However, the Israelites had personally witnessed the many miracles of the Exodus, and this is something to which they could relate. Once they had had a sensory experience of the existence of Hashem, they could base their *emunah* on that.

Many philosophers have tried to utilize reasoning to prove the existence of God, but it is possible to refute their arguments. Trying to think logically about God is frustrating. Our *emunah* is based on an unbroken transmission of the Revelation at Sinai, which was witnessed by millions of people.

Kabbalistic books often refer to Hashem as being *ein sof*, without end. This is all one can say about the essence of Hashem. We can talk about whatever He has revealed of Himself to us, but we must realize that His eternity, His "I am the first and I am the last," is beyond our ability to grasp.

So said Hashem ... I am the first and I am the last.

R' Shneur Zalman was a disciple of the Maggid of Mezeritch. One day, he was struggling to understand a difficult portion of the Talmud, and sought the Maggid's elucidation. He knocked on the Maggid's door.
 "Who's there?" asked the Maggid.
 "It is I," R' Shneur responded.
 "It is you, Zalman? Come in."

After explaining the Talmud, the Maggid said, "Fohr gezunterheit!" (Travel in good health!). R' Shneur was bewildered. He had no intention of leaving. But, since the Maggid had said "Fohr gezunterheit," he had to leave, but he had no idea whereto. "Fohr" implies to travel by some means, but he had no money to hire a horse and wagon. Therefore, he took his tallis and tefillin and left Mezeritch on foot.

As he walked along the countryside, he heard someone calling to him, "Reb Yid! You must be none other than the prophet Elijah himself. We have a bris [circumcision] here, and we have only nine men. You are the tenth needed for the minyan. Please join us."

R' Shneur Zalman joined the group. After the bris had been performed, they welcomed him to join the festive meal. After the meal had ended, the hostess counted the silverware, and one silver spoon was missing. The men turned to R' Shneur Zalman. "We appreciate your completing our minyan, but that does not justify your stealing a silver spoon. If you need tzedakah, we will gladly help you, but you must return the spoon."

R' Shneur Zalman said, "I did not take a silver spoon."

The men said angrily, "Of course you did. We all know each other. No one could have taken it except you. Don't try to deny it."

R' Shneur Zalman said, "No, not I."

The men then beat him. "Give back the spoon! You are a thief!"

R' Shneur Zalman said, "No, not I."

The men continued to beat him mercilessly, saying, "It was you!" and R' Shneur Zalman continued protesting, "No, not I."

One of the kitchen help, who had taken the spoon, could not tolerate seeing an innocent person being beaten mercilessly, and she confessed to having taken the spoon. The men apologized to R' Shneur Zalman, who forgave them and left the village.

R' Shneur Zalman reasoned, "The purpose the Rebbe had for sending me away is because I deserved a punishment. Now that I've been beaten, that was accomplished, so I may now return."

When he returned to Mezeritch, the Maggid was awaiting him and said, "Zalman, when I asked you, 'Who's there?' you said, 'It is I.' Only Hashem has the right to say 'It is I.' A human being should be self-effacing and not think of himself as 'I.' So, for the one time you said, 'It is I,' you had to compensate by saying many times, 'Not I.' Remember, the Ten Commandments begin with 'I am the Lord, your God.' Only Hashem may say, 'It is I.'"

The eighth verse in *Malchios* is:

And the saviors will ascend Mount Zion to judge the mountain of Esau and the kingdom will be Hashem's (Obadiah 1:21).

According to *Radak*, the "saviors" are Mashiach and the seven "shepherds" (Abraham, Isaac, Jacob, Moses, Aaron, Joseph, and David) who will accompany Mashiach at the Redemption. They will eliminate evil, as personified by Esau, and the universal sovereignty of Hashem will then be acknowledged by all nations.

The ninth verse in *Malchios* is:

> ***Then Hashem will be King over all the land, on that day Hashem will be One and His Name will be One (Zechariah 14:9).***

The idol worshipers initially realized that there was a God Who had created the world, but believed that He was so lofty that it was beneath His dignity to concern Himself with the conduct of Earth. He, therefore, turned over the day-to-day operation of the world to subordinates, whom they began to worship. With the Redemption, all peoples will recognize that Hashem alone controls the world.

Ibn Ezra says that "His Name will be One" refers to the fact that we do not pronounce the Tetragrammaton, the Name of Hashem as it is written, but instead we say "A-do-noi." After the Redemption, we will be permitted to say the Name of Hashem as it is written.

The tenth verse in *Malchios* is:

> ***And in Your Torah it is written, "Hear, O Israel, Hashem is our God, Hashem is the One and Only" (Deuteronomy 6:4).***

This verse hardly requires comment. If we were to elaborate on it, it would necessitate an entire volume to cite all the commentary.

Our belief in the Oneness of Hashem is the foundation of our entire faith.

> *R' Zushe of Anipole said to his brother, R' Elimelech of Lizhensk, "Melech, we are told that all the neshamos for all time to come were found in the neshamah of Adam. That means that your neshamah and mine were there, too. How did we let Adam eat of the Tree of Knowledge that Hashem had forbidden?"*
>
> *R' Elimelech said, "Not only did I not stop him from eating it, I actually encouraged it. You see, the serpent told Adam, 'God knows that if you eat from this tree, you will be as great as He is.' If Adam had not eaten from that tree, for the rest of his life he would have harbored the heretical thought, 'If I had eaten from that tree, I could have been equal to God.' I thought, 'It is better that he should eat from the tree and know that no one can be equal to Hashem.'"*

Hear, O Israel, Hashem is Elokeinu [our God], Hashem is the One and Only.

As we have often noted, in Kabbalah it says that the Name of God, *Hashem*, refers to His conducting the world with the trait of *chesed* (kindness). The Name *Elokim* (translated as God) refers to His conducting the world with *din* (strict judgment). Nonetheless, we believe that what we experience as *din* is in fact *chesed*, even if we do not see it as such.

When a mother restrains her infant to enable the doctor to give him an immunizing injection, the infant cannot possibly understand why the mother who loves and protects him is collaborating with this terrible person who stabs him. The infant has no way of knowing that it is the mother's love for him that makes her do this, to protect him from potentially fatal diseases. Nor can we understand why Hashem allows painful things to happen to us.

So we say, *Hashem, Elokeinu, Hashem echad;* both Names of God manifest *chesed*, and *chesed* cloaked in *din* is all *Hashem echad*, all *chesed*. However, because with our human perception we do not see it that way, we cover our eyes to express our belief that our human perception is faulty, and our *emunah* is firm in Hashem's *chesed*.

We close the *Malchios* segment with the prayer that includes the following verse:

> *Let everything that has been made know that You are its Maker, let everything that has been molded understand that You are its Molder ....*

> *R' Mendel of Rimanov was walking with his disciples, and they came across a child who was crying. R' Mendel asked the child what was wrong, and the child said, "We are playing hide-and-seek. I hid myself, but no one is coming to look for me."*
>
> *R' Mendel turned to his disciples. "Hashem has concealed Himself in the world. Can you understand His great distress when no one is looking for Him?"*

We pray for the day when people will realize that Hashem is everywhere but has concealed Himself in nature, and they will seek to find Him.

☞ *Zichronos*

True, the Talmud quotes Hashem as saying, "Recite *Zichronos* before Me, that your remembrances will come before Me." However, we know that Hashem does not need to be reminded of anything.

As we say *Zichronos*, we should bear in mind the closing words of this segment, "For it is You Who eternally remembers all forgotten things …." The commentaries say, "That which a person forgets, Hashem remembers. That which a person remembers, Hashem forgets."

King David says, "My sin is always before me" (*Psalms* 51:5). Let us take a moment to analyze this verse.

The prophet says, "I will have wiped away your willful sins like a thick mist and your transgressions like a cloud; return to Me, for I will have redeemed you" (*Isaiah* 44:22). When a fog clears, there is no trace of it, and when Hashem forgives our sins, there is no trace of them, as we say in *Tashlich*, "And all the sins of Your nation, the House of Israel, cast away to a place where they will neither be remembered, considered, nor brought to mind — ever." In light of this, what does David mean by stating, "My sin is always before me"?

In addition to meaning "sin," the word *chet* also means "lack" or "defect." A sin can only occur in a person who has a lack of *yiras Shamayim*, which rendered him vulnerable to committing that sin. Even after the sin is forgiven, a person should always remember that he had that vulnerability, and should forever be on his guard. Although the sin is erased through *teshuvah*, a person should not forget that he has been swayed in the past.

"That which a person remembers, Hashem forgets." If a person remembers his susceptibility to sin, Hashem forgets the sin. "That which a person forgets, Hashem remembers." If a person treats his sin lightly and totally dismisses it from his mind, he indicates that he is not sincere in his dedication to Hashem, and Hashem will remember this.

Tzaddikim always feel that they fall short of proper service of Hashem. They do not retain memory of their mitzvos, because, in their humility, they feel that their mitzvos were imperfect. Hashem remembers these mitzvos. However, if a person thinks himself to be a *tzaddik* by virtue of the mitzvos he performed, this is a sign of vanity, and Hashem pays little attention to such mitzvos. Thus, "That which a person forgets, Hashem remembers. That which a person remembers, Hashem forgets."

Let us analyze the segment on *Zichronos*.

> ***Regarding countries, it is said on this day which is destined for the sword and which for peace.***

The Maggid of Warsaw related a parable.

> *A nobleman had a beautiful garden consisting of many trees and flowers. He also had placed numerous statues throughout the garden. In the event of heavy rain, his servant would move the statues into an airtight and waterproof shed.*
>
> *One day, several visitors toured the garden, and enjoyed the trees and flowers. Suddenly, a heavy rain fell, and the servant hastened to move the statues into the shed. He said to the visitors, "Follow me, and you'll*

be out of the rain." He then led them into the shed and closed the door.

Soon the visitors began pounding on the door. "Let us out!"

The servant said, "You're better off in the shed. It protects the statues from the rain, so it will protect you."

The visitors said, "You fool! We'll suffocate in here. The statues don't breathe. We need air!"

When we see some nations prosper while the Jewish nation is poor, we should realize that it is because those nations have no need for Torah and mitzvos. For Jews, Torah and mitzvos are our oxygen, and if we don't observe them, we will suffocate.

Praiseworthy is the man who does not forget You.

R' Yaakov Yitzchak (the Yehudi HaKodesh) once found the Chozeh (Seer) of Lublin to be in low spirits. "What is bothering the master?" he asked.

"I realize that I have transgressed the warning, 'Be cautious lest you forget Hashem.' (Deuteronomy 6:12). For a moment, I was not thinking of Hashem."

The Yehudi HaKodesh said, "The master has no need to worry. The halachah is that if a person forgets a sheaf of grain in the field, he must leave it for the poor. (This is the mitzvah of "shikchah.") However, if it is an unusually large sheaf, the mitzvah of shikchah does not apply. He certainly could not have forgotten it, and it was somewhere in the recesses of his mind

[Peah 6:6]. Hashem is so great that the master could not have forgotten Him, and He was somewhere in your mind."

The Seer said, "You have restored me to life."

The first verse regarding *Zichronos* is:

> **God remembered Noah and all the beasts and all the animals that were with him in the Ark, and God caused a spirit to pass over the earth, and the waters subsided (Genesis 8:1).**

What was the great merit of Noah? Ohr HaChaim says that it was his indefatigable care of the animals. Indeed, Noah was once harmed when a lion kicked him because he did not feed it on time.

The Torah is very concerned about compassion for animals. The Talmud says that R' Yehudah HaNasi (the Prince) was in the House of Study when a calf that was being led to the slaughterhouse ran away and hid under his cloak. R' Yehudah said, "Go! This is what you were created for." Because of his lack of compassion for the calf, he was afflicted with pain. Indeed, the Talmud says that a person should not sit down to a meal until he has fed his animals (*Berachos* 40a).

> *One Rosh Hashanah, the worshipers noticed that R' Moshe Leib of Sasov was not in the shul. They found him watering and feeding the horses.*
>
> *He explained, "Everyone is so occupied with davening that the animals were hungry and thirsty."*

The second verse in *Zichronos* is:

> **God heard their moaning, and God remembered His**
> **covenant with Abraham, with Isaac, and with Jacob**
> **(Exodus 2:24).**

The verse in the Torah immediately preceding this is, "The children of Israel groaned *because of the work* and they cried out. Their outcry *because of the work* went up to God" (ibid. 2:23). The phrase, "because of the work," is repeated. The Hebrew for this phrase is *"min ha'avodah,"* which Chassidic writers say can also refer to *avodas Hashem* (serving Hashem). The Israelites groaned not only because of the hard work they were forced to do, but also because they were unable to serve Hashem.

> *There were two neighbors, one a fine talmid chacham*
> *(Torah scholar) who would arise early in the morning,*
> *study Torah, daven at length, and return to his Torah*
> *study. His neighbor was a simple, unlearned person, who*
> *arose early in the morning and davened quickly to be*
> *able to get to work on time. During the day he would*
> *recite the chapters of Tehillim that he knew by heart.*
> *Whenever he saw his talmid chacham neighbor, he*
> *envied the latter's ability to study Torah and to daven*
> *leisurely, and he would groan that he was not fortunate*
> *to serve Hashem in this manner.*
>
> *When they came before the Heavenly Tribunal, the*
> *talmid chacham was rewarded for his devotion to Torah*
> *and tefillah. The unlearned person's Torah and tefillah*
> *were meager, but the angels added all his heartfelt*

— 175 —

*groans that he was not fortunate to serve Hashem like
his neighbor, and the Heavenly Tribunal gave him a
portion of Gan Eden equal to that of his neighbor.*

Because the Israelites groaned not only because of their hard work, but also because they could not devote adequate time to *avodas Hashem,* Hashem remembered that they were the children of Abraham, Isaac, and Jacob, who were totally devoted to Hashem. Their descendants, too, were devoted to Hashem, but their bitter enslavement did not allow them to express their devotion. These groans earned their deliverance.

R' Yisrael Salanter asked, according to the opinion that we have exhausted the merits of Abraham, Isaac, and Jacob (*Shabbos* 55a), how do we still invoke them now? R' Yisrael answered with a parable.

*There was a very wealthy man who owned farms and
factories. When he died, his spendthrift son squandered
all the money of his inheritance. However, the farms and
factories continued to be productive and generate income.*

In addition to their great merits, Abraham, Isaac, and Jacob taught us how to live a Torah life and how to do mitzvos. Even if we have used up their "cash" merits, we still have the merits of the "farms and factories" — the mitzvos that they taught us to do.

The third verse in *Zichronos* is:

**I will remember My covenant with Jacob, and also
My covenant with Isaac, and also My covenant with
Abraham will I remember, and I will remember the
Land (Leviticus 26:42).**

Why are the Patriarchs mentioned in reverse order? The Maggid of Dubnow explained with a parable.

> *A young boy bought a pound of candy, and after the proprietor gave him the bag, he said, "Here are a few more."*
>
> *Another boy, who saw this transaction, said, "You gave him candy that he did not pay for. Give me some, too."*
>
> *The proprietor said, "No way! He bought a whole pound of candy, so I gave him a bonus. You didn't buy anything. Why should I give you any for free?"*

Similarly, if we would have begun with Abraham and Isaac's merits, Ishmael and Esau would have said, "We are also descendants of Abraham and Isaac. Give us some of their merits, too." Therefore, Hashem began with Jacob, who established the Jewish nation with the twelve tribes, and his merits suffice to give them the Land of Israel. To this, we add the merits of Abraham and Isaac as a bonus.

The fourth verse in *Zichronos* is:

> **He made a memorial for His wonders, gracious and compassionate is Hashem (Psalms 111:4).**

When we kindle the lights on Chanukah and read the Megillah on Purim, we recite the *berachah,* "Who has wrought miracles for our forefathers, in those days at this season." The Ari *z"l* says that when Hashem performs a miracle for Israel, the day of the year on which the miracle occurred becomes favorable for kindnesses from Hashem every year. That is why we stress "at this season" in the *berachah*, to remind us that the days of Chanukah and Purim are favorable days for us.

Yosef Tehillos states that this is what the verse in *Psalms* is referring to: Hashem memorialized the days of His wonders, perpetuating them to provide extra compassion and mercy to Israel.

The fifth verse in *Zichronos* is:

> *He provided food for those who fear Him. He eternally*
> *remembers His covenant (Psalms 111:5).*

Imros Tehoros states that Hashem provides for us even if we personally have not been deserving. He does so by virtue of our forefathers who feared Him. As noted above, the Talmud cites an opinion that we may exhaust the merits of our forefathers (*Shabbos* 55a). The psalmist says, "Even if the merits of the Patriarchs should be depleted, Hashem will continue to provide for us by virtue of His covenant with them, which is eternal."

The sixth verse in *Zichronos* is:

> *He remembered His covenant for them and relented,*
> *in accordance with His abundant kindness*
> *(Psalms 106:45).*

We can be assured that our *teshuvah* will be accepted because Hashem's kindnesses are indeed abundant, and His desire to forgive us is overwhelming.

Psalm 106 relates how the Israelites repeatedly deviated from Hashem's will, and after Hashem accepted their *teshuvah* and helped them, they relapsed.

A human being would not tolerate repeated relapses, and would not accept a person's remorse as being sincere. But Hashem's *middos* are not like those of mortals. In spite of one's failure to keep his promises to behave properly, Hashem again and again accepts our *teshuvah*. He will do so again this year, and inscribe us in the Book of Life.

The seventh verse in *Zichronos* is:

> *Go and call out in the ears of Jerusalem, saying: Thus said Hashem: I remember for your sake the kindness of your youth, the love of your nuptials, your following Me into the Wilderness, into an unsown land (Jeremiah 2:2).*

R' Levi Yitzchak of Berditchev says that we have a reciprocal relationship of praise with Hashem. We refer to Passover as "Pesach," because Hashem passed over the homes of Jews when He smote the Egyptian firstborn, but Hashem refers to Passover in the Torah as *Chag HaMatzos,* emphasizing that we left Egypt in such haste that we did not have time to make provisions (*Exodus* 12:39), following Moses with blind faith.

We repeatedly mention the Exodus from Egypt in our services. This is both to praise Hashem for His deliverance and to invoke the pure faith of our ancestors, who did not ask "What will we eat in the desert?"

The eighth verse in *Zichronos* is:

> *But I will remember My covenant [made] with you of the days of your youth, and I will establish for you an everlasting covenant (Ezekiel 16:60).*

The Torah says that even though Israel may deviate from Hashem's will, "... despite all this [their sinfulness] ... I will not have been revolted by them...for I am Hashem, their God. I will remember for them the covenant of the ancients ..." (*Leviticus* 26:44-45). Hashem assures us that His love for Israel and His relationship with us is eternal and unconditional.

The ninth verse in *Zichronos* is:

> *Is Ephraim My most precious son or a delightful child, that whenever I speak of him I remember him more and more? Therefore My inner self yearns for him, I will surely take pity on him — these are the words of Hashem (Jeremiah 31:19).*

I have a special affinity for this verse, which refers to the ten tribes of Israel who were driven into exile because of their impetuous behavior. I have seen many cases of young men and women whose behavior was so self-destructive and who would not accept corrective guidance, that their parents had no other option but to tell them, "If you cannot stop your irresponsible and rash behavior, you cannot remain in this house." There is nothing more painful in the world than for a parent to evict a child, and I can understand Hashem's distress in sending His children into exile.

Although the parent may be angry at the child, the parent's love for the child never diminishes, and he prays for the child's well-being, never losing hope that the child will abandon his harmful ways and return.

Hashem's yearning for His children is even greater than that of parents for their child.

> **Remember for us, Hashem, the covenant, the kindness, and the oath that You swore to our father Abraham on Mount Moriah.**

These are words of the *machzor* but are not a verse in Scripture. The Maggid of Dubnow commented:

When he was already advanced in years, a man was blessed with a child. When the man neared death, the son was only nine years old. The father asked a friend to look after the son and designated the friend to be trustee of his estate.

The trustee executed his duty faithfully. He cared for the lad and saw to it that he learned a trade. When the young man turned twenty, the trustee told him that his father had left him a substantial sum of money.

The son said, "That's great! I don't have to go to work any more. I can live a life of leisure."

The trustee said, "Yes, you can. You are now of age and I must turn the money over to you. But if you don't work now and instead squander all the money, then you won't have any when you marry and want to buy a house and provide for the needs of your family. I suggest you leave the money in the bank and go to work."

So it is with us. Abraham left us his many merits, but we would be foolish to fritter them away. We would be wise to "go to work" and earn our own merits by doing mitzvos.

The tenth verse in *Zichronos* is:

> *I shall remember for them the covenant of the ancient ones, those whom I have taken out of the land of Egypt before the eyes of the nations, to be God unto them — I am Hashem (Leviticus 26:45).*

R' Levi Yitzchak of Berditchev, always the advocate for Israel, cited the verse, "Remember Your congregation, which You acquired long ago, You redeemed the tribe of Your heritage ..." (*Psalms* 74:2), and related this parable.

> *A man made a shidduch (marriage match) for his son with the daughter of a person who had the reputation of being wealthy. It subsequently was revealed that the prospective father-in-law was impoverished and hopelessly in debt. The man moved to annul the shidduch on the basis that he had been misinformed.*
>
> *However, if he had made a shidduch with a person who was known to be penniless, he would not be permitted to seek to break the shidduch because the girl's father has no money. "You knew that all along," he will be told.*

R' Levi Yitzchak cited the Ari *z"l's* statement that the reason Hashem took the Children of Israel out of Egypt with such great haste (*Deuteronomy* 16:3) was because they were in so profound a state of contamination that if they had remained in Egypt one more moment, they would have been beyond salvation. R' Levi Yitzchak said, "When You took us for a nation, we were in a very poor spiritual state. You cannot, therefore, disown us if we are not as spiritual as You would like us to be."

And so we say, "Remember for them the covenant of the early ones, those whom You took out of the land of Egypt." We are surely more spiritual now than we were then.

☞ Shofros

As was noted, the Talmud quotes Hashem as saying, "Recite verses of *Malchios* (Kingship) before Me, so that you enthrone Me over yourselves. Recite verses of *Zichronos* (memories) before Me, so that your memories come before Me, And with what? With the shofar" (*Rosh Hashanah* 16a, 34b). Obviously, just reciting the verses of *Malchios* and *Zichronos* would not be enough. The shofar is the vehicle that effectuates the verse that brings about the coronation and the memories. What is the power of the shofar?

As was noted in the commentary on Psalm 47, there are two attitudes necessary for *avodas Hashem*. *Simchah* is all important, as the psalmist says, "Serve Hashem with gladness" (*Psalms* 100:2). But one must also be aware of his shortcomings and sins, and the broken-heartedness of this awareness is desirable, as the psalmist says, "A heart broken and humbled, O God, You will not despise" (ibid. 51:19). That these two attitudes can coexist are evident in the psalmist's statement, "Rejoice amidst trembling" (ibid 2:11). One attitude without the other is incomplete.

When we enthrone Hashem, we should be euphoric that He is our King and we are His subjects, but that also makes us aware of how remiss we have been in serving Him. The memories that come before Hashem are both of the mitzvos we have performed and of the sins we have committed. We must be cognizant of all these attitudes and feelings.

The shofar symbolizes the compatibility of these feelings. It is a wailing sound, expressing our broken-heartedness, but it is also a sound of triumph and freedom. On the Yom Kippur of *Yovel* (Jubilee), slaves are emancipated and properties returned to their original owners with the sounding of the shofar.

Both *malchios* and *zichronos* are dependent on the shofar.

The first verse in *Shofros* is:

> ***On the third day when it was morning,***
> ***there was thunder and lightning,***
> ***and a heavy cloud on the mountain,***
> ***and the sound of the shofar was very powerful,***
> ***and the entire people that was in the camp trembled***
> ***(Exodus 19:16).***

We are required to recall the revelation of Sinai every day. Indeed, in the *siddur*, the six constant remembrances are listed at the end of the *Shacharis* service. One of them states, "Only beware for yourself and guard yourself carefully, lest you forget the things your eyes have seen and lest they stray from your heart all the days of your life. And you are to make them known to your children and to your children's children — the day you stood before Hashem, your God, at Horeb" (*Deuteronomy* 4:9-10).

R' Shlomo Wolbe, in *Alei Shur,* says that we are required to use our imagination and picture the scene in our minds: Millions of Jews standing at the foot of Mount Sinai, the mountain aflame and trembling; millions of Jews hearing the lightning and seeing the thunder, hearing the shofar, and seeing Moses standing at the top of the mountain, ready to receive the words of Hashem. What our ancestors saw with their eyes and heard with their ears, we are to achieve with our imagination.

The second verse in *Shofros* is:

> *The sound of the shofar grew continually much stronger; Moses would speak and Hashem would respond to him with a voice (Exodus 19:19).*

Klei Yakar makes an interesting comment. There were two sensory experiences at Sinai: thunder and lightning and the shofar. The difference between the two was that thunder and lightning were fleeting experiences: thunder lasting for a second or two, and lightning even less than that.

These represent two experiences in Torah study. There are those who have a brief inspiration to learn Torah, but it soon dissipates, like the momentary thunder and lightning. There are serious students of Torah, whose interest in Torah grows progressively stronger, like the sound of the shofar.

The shofar on Rosh Hashanah teaches us to constantly seek to increase our knowledge and understanding of and our devotion to Torah study.

The third verse in *Shofros* is:

> *The entire people saw the thunder and the flames, and the sound of the shofar and the smoking mountain; and the people saw and trembled and they stood from afar (Exodus 20:15).*

"They saw the sounds." Rashi cites the Midrash stating that

there was a miracle whereby they saw what is usually only audible. The Rebbe of Kotzk asked, "What purpose did this miracle serve?"

The Rebbe answered, "The Hebrew word, *lo*, when spelled *lamed-vav*, means "to him" or "for him." When spelled *lamed-aleph*, *lo* means "no." However, both share the identical pronunciation.

Had the Israelites only heard, "*lo signov* — you shall not steal," they might have misunderstood the *lo signov* as meaning "for Him you may steal," which would justify stealing in order to do a mitzvah, such as stealing an *esrog* or stealing money to give to *tzedakah*. Therefore, they had to see the sounds, to see that *lo* was written *lamed-aleph*, that there is never any justification for stealing.

Giving *tzedakah* with money that is acquired dishonestly is not a mitzvah.

The fourth verse in *Shofros* is:

> ***God has ascended with the blast; Hashem, with the sound of the shofar (Psalms 47:6).***

As we noted earlier the interpretation of the word *teruah* means "friendship," and that Hashem ascends from the Throne of Judgment to the Throne of Mercy when there is friendship and unity among Jews. The Maggid of Mezeritch said that it also means that we arouse Hashem's mercy when we perform the mitzvos, such as shofar, with an attitude of *teruah*, "friendship," and love for Hashem.

The fifth verse in *Shofros* is:

> ***With trumpets and shofar sound, call out before the King, Hashem (Psalms 98:6).***

Trumpets are sounded on joyous occasions. "On the day of your gladness, and on your festivals, and on your new moons, you shall sound the trumpets ..." (*Numbers* 10:10). The shofar's *teruah*, as we have seen, is a sound of groaning or weeping, in pain or grief.

The Talmud says that a person is required to praise Hashem for adverse happenings just as well as for good happenings (*Berachos* 54a). This verse teaches us that both with trumpets (happy occasions) and shofar (*teruah*= adversities), we should call out our praises to Hashem (*Shaarei Chaim*).

The sixth verse in *Shofros* is:

> *Blow the shofar at the moon's renewal, at the time*
> *appointed for our festive day. Because it is a decree for*
> *Israel, a judgment [day] for the God of Jacob*
> *(Psalms 81:4-5).*

R' Levi Yitzchak of Berditchev cites the *Zohar*, who is critical of self-centered prayers asking only for one's needs. R' Levi Yitzchak states that just as a father is happy when he can fulfill his child's desires, so too, Hashem is pleased when He can bestow His kindnesses on His children. The ideal intention when praying for our needs and desires is that fulfilling our requests will give Hashem pleasure. However, Hashem operates within the confines of justice. If we have sinned and are not deserving of Hashem's kindnesses, Hashem will not usurp His principles of justice.

The prosecuting angels wish to bring our sins before Hashem, but that may result in frustrating, so to speak, Hashem's desires to give to us. Knowing that Hashem will be displeased with them for hampering His desires to give to us, the prosecuting angels may actually refrain from doing so.

"This," said R' Levi Yitzchak, "may be the meaning of the above verse. 'A decree for Israel' is a judgment day *for Hashem Himself,* Whose wish to give to us can be realized depending on whether or not we receive a favorable decree."

We now recite Psalm 150, because the Talmud says that the ten verses of each segment, *Malchios, Zichronos, Shofros,* correspond to the ten times the word *hallelu* (praise) is found in this chapter (*Likutei Maharich*).

The seventh verse in *Shofros* is:

> *All inhabitants of the world and dwellers of the earth — you will see [that Israel has been ingathered] when the banner is hoisted upon the mountain, and when the shofar sounds, you will hear! (Isaiah 18:3).*

This is prophecy of the Ultimate Redemption as it is expressed in the next verse.

The eighth verse in *Shofros* is:

> *It shall be on that day that a great shofar will be blown, and those who are lost in the land of Assyria and those cast away in the land of Egypt will come [together]; and they will prostrate themselves to Hashem on the holy mountain in Jerusalem (Isaiah 27:13).*

Although we have not yet merited the fulfillment of this prophecy, we are fortunate in witnessing so many young people who were "lost" and "cast away" returning to *Yiddishkeit* and to Torah study. Some of these have experimented with all manner of religions, and have come back to their roots in Judaism. Some have published the stories of their journeys away from and of their return to the faith of their forefathers. These narratives testify to their disillusion in the search for meaning in life in other venues. It is heartening to see them at the *Kosel* (Western Wall), and realize that they have truly come to "prostrate themselves to Hashem on the holy mountain in Jerusalem."

The ninth verse in *Shofros* is:

> *Hashem will appear to them, and His arrow will go forth like the lightning; and the Lord, Hashem/Elokim will blow with a shofar and go forth in southern tempests. Hashem, Master of Legions, will protect them (Zechariah 9:14-15).*

This verse has been variously interpreted to refer to Hashem's doing battle against the enemies of Israel before the Ultimate Redemption or to the triumph of the Hasmoneans over the Syrian Greeks during the conflict culminating in Chanukah.

The tenth verse in *Shofros* is:

> *On the day of your gladness, and on your festivals, and on your new moons you shall sound the trumpets over your burnt-offerings and over your feast peace-offerings; and they shall be a remembrance for you before your God; I am Hashem your God (Numbers 10:10).*

To what does "the day of your gladness" refer? *Sifri* says that this refers to Shabbos. This is the only place where we find Shabbos cited as a day of *simchah* (joy). Shabbos is indeed a joyous day, but we must do our part to make it so.

One of the beloved *zemiros* (Shabbos songs) is *Menuchah V'simchah* (tranquility and gladness). Other peoples have a day of rest, but for them it is a day on which to recharge their batteries so that they can work for the upcoming six days; this makes the day of rest subordinate to the workweek. Shabbos is different. In the morning service on Sunday we say, "Today is the first day toward Shabbos." On Monday we say, "Today is the second day toward Shabbos," etc. The entire week is directed toward Shabbos.

Shabbos is a spiritual day, a day that should be devoted to prayer and Torah study, to strengthening our bonds with family and friends. Shabbos gives meaning to the workweek and to life itself. Properly observed, Shabbos is a day of *simchah*.

A person who observes Shabbos is referred to as a *shomer Shabbos*. The word *shomer* also means "to guard; to protect." It has been aptly said that even more than Jews have been *shomer Shabbos* (observant of Shabbos), Shabbos has been *shomer Yisrael* (protector and guardian of Israel). It is a truly a day of tranquility and gladness.

Shofros closes with the phrase, "For You hear the sound of the shofar and You give ear to the *teruah* and none is comparable to You ...."

What is the relevance of the words "none is comparable to You" at this juncture?

Earlier, in the section on sounding the shofar, we noted the verse, "Praises to the people who know the shofar's cry; Hashem, by the illumination of Your countenance they walk" (*Psalms* 89:16), and the Midrashic comment, "Is Israel the only people that know how to blow the shofar? Why, all the nations have musicians who play musical instruments! What the psalmist means is, 'Praises to the people who know how to appease their Creator with the shofar blast'" (*Vayikra Rabbah* 29). We know how to appease Hashem, and Hashem knows how to listen to us.

There is a reciprocal relationship between Hashem and Israel. In the *tefillin* we have verses that cite the praise of Hashem. The Talmud says that Hashem, too, dons *tefillin,* in which it says, "Who is like Your people, Israel, a unique nation on the earth (*Berachos* 6a).

The Torah says, "You have distinguished Hashem today to be a God to you … and Hashem has distinguished you today to be for Him (see *Deuteronomy* 26:17-18).

> *R' Levi Yitzchak of Berditchev heard a man davening, mumbling the words so that they were unintelligible. R' Levi Yitzchak spoke to the man, also mumbling unintelligibly.*
>
> *"I can't understand what you are saying," the man said.*
>
> *R' Levi Yitzchak respnded, "I am talking to you in the same way you talk to Hashem."*
>
> *The man said, "Rebbe, when an infant makes unintelligible sounds, no one can understand him. However, the parents know what these sounds mean and what the infant wants. Hashem is a father. He understands what I am saying."*

R' Levi Yitzchak, a devoted advocate for Israel, was overjoyed with the man's explanation.

Anyone can hear the sound of the shofar, but only Hashem knows the thoughts and feelings we put into the sounding of the shofar. This is why we say, "For You hear the sound of the shofar and You give ear to the *teruah* and *none is comparable to You.*" Everyone can hear the sound of the shofar, but only Hashem understands it.

Mussaf: Chazzan's Repetition

☞ The Authority of the Sages

> *Based on the tradition of our wise and discerning*
> *teachers, and the teaching derived from the knowledge*
> *of the discerning, I open my mouth in prayer and*
> *supplications to beseech and beg favor before the King*
> *Who reigns over kings and the Master of masters.*

Earlier, we cited justification for listing additional praise of Hashem and not being subject to R' Chanina's chastisement, "Have you exhausted all the praises of your Master." One more justification is the principle stated by Rashi (*Genesis* 7:1) that in the imminent presence of another, one does not say all that person's praises. The *chazzan* says he will beg favor *pnei Melech Malchei hamelachim* — in the immediate presence of Hashem. Therefore, he may list only partial praises.

As was noted earlier, our practice, following the opinion of Rema (*Orach Chaim* 68, 112), is to include *piyutim* in the Amidah, and the *chazzan* declares that we do so by virtue of the authority of our wise and discerning Torah scholars. This assures the congregation that these additions are in full accord with Torah theology.

☞ *Liturgical Poems*

אָפֵּד מֵאָז
Established From Yore

As noted earlier, Rosh Hashanah commemorates not the first day of Creation, but rather the sixth day, the day Adam was created. This *piyut* refers to Adam, who was given a single prohibition by Hashem, and, within hours, transgressed it. Although it appears that Hashem told him that he would die on the day he ate the forbidden fruit, the *Targum Yonasan ben Uziel* translates the words, "On the day you will eat of it *you will deserve death*" (*Genesis* 2:17). Therefore, Hashem commuted Adam's sentence, punished him by banishing him from the Garden of Eden, and inflicted upon him a life of suffering. The day on which Hashem was merciful to Adam is the day on which all humanity is judged, and we invoke the mercy shown to Adam in our favor.

The sin of Adam has far-reaching consequences, not in that we are tainted with his sin, but that we unwisely duplicate it in our own lives. Adam's sin has a long-lasting influence, not so much because we are still punished for it, but because we have apparently not learned from it and we continue to repeat it.

What was Adam's sin? Hashem told him that the fruit of the Tree of Knowledge is forbidden, and that if he eats it he will die. What did the serpent say? "Don't worry. You won't die." And so,

Eve saw that the fruit looked delicious; she gave in to temptation and ate it. She believed the serpent that convinced her that Hashem's words constituted an empty threat. Many people are still like that. "Cigarettes cause cancer, but it won't happen to me." People ignore the warning signs about addiction; they don't believe that the disasters can happen to them.

The Midrash says that Hashem gave Adam a tour of Gan Eden and said, "I created all this for you. Take heed that you don't ruin My world, because there will be no one to rectify it" (*Koheles Rabbah* 9). Yet, because of lucrative development and industrial profits, we pollute the air and water, destroy the rain forests, and wipe out species.

Adam was forgiven by the merits of his descendants, the Patriarchs and Matriarchs. We, too, invoke their merits in our judgment.

מֶלֶךְ עֶלְיוֹן
The Supreme King

The Ark is opened and we chant the following *piyut*.

This beautiful liturgical poem, which is often sung by the entire congregation with an upbeat melody, is not only a praise of Hashem, His noble attributes, and His infinite might, but it also contrasts Him with earthly monarchs, who, despite their lofty status, are mere mortals, ultimately powerless to save themselves.

Initially, each verse lauding Hashem was followed by a verse describing the inconsequential status of a human monarch. There is reason to believe that for fear that temporal rulers might take offense, most of the stanzas referring to mortal monarchs were deleted. Only two were retained, and these are recited in an undertone, with the Ark closed.

The inspiration for this poem may have been Chapter 14 of *Isaiah*, wherein the prophet chides Nebuchadnezzar, who said, "I will ascend to the heavens; higher than the stars of God I shall raise my throne .... I will ascend over the tops of the clouds; I will liken myself to the Most High" (*Isaiah* 14:13-14). Yet Nebuchadnezzar died an ignominious death and, in contrast to other kings, was not even afforded a respectable burial.

"*Melech Elyon*" is at once a beautiful praise of Hashem and an admonishment that people who may have attained positions of prestige and power should not allow their egos to be inflated by virtue of their superior social status.

Nesivos Shalom raises the question, "Of what value are the praises of mere mortals to Hashem, Who is infinite? He answers that whereas words are the expression of the mind, song is the expression of the heart. This is why *shirah* has so important a role in *Yiddishkeit*. A person sings to his beloved because his heart overflows with emotion, and song is the most effective method of expressing his feelings. This is why *Shir HaShirim* (*Song of Songs*) is considered the Holiest of the Holiest (*Sanhedrin* 101a), because it attests to our intense love for Hashem. Similarly, the praises in "*Melech Elyon*" express our *deveikus* — our desire to be close to Hashem — and our intense love for Him.

וּנְתַנֶּה תֹּקֶף קְדֻשַׁת הַיּוֹם, כִּי הוּא נוֹרָא וְאָים
Let Us Now Relate the Power of This Day's Holiness

This prayer is one of the most stirring compositions in the entire liturgy of Rosh Hashanah and Yom Kippur. It is recited before the opened Ark. It was composed by R' Amnon of Mainz,

Germany, about one thousand years ago. This is the story behind it:

> *R' Amnon of Mainz, Germany was a confidant of the bishop of that city. As a result of this relationship, during the week before Rosh Hashanah, the bishop exhorted R' Amnon to convert to Christianity. The bishop was most adamant and would not take no for an answer.*
>
> *In an effort to delay having to give a definitive response, R' Amnon requested a three-day grace period in which to weigh his options. His petition was granted. However, when he reached his residence, R' Amnon was in a frenzy. How could he possible have sunk to such depths as to allow the bishop to think that he might reject Hashem and His Torah?*
>
> *For three days, R' Anmon immersed himself in prayer and abstained from eating in penance for his misdeed. When the three days had passed, he did not appear before the bishop. Angry and annoyed, the bishop had R' Amnon brought before him and demanded a response.*
>
> *R' Amnon did not yield before this ultimatum. His only reply was that his tongue should be cut out, since it was the vehicle whereby he had uttered his ill-advised request for time, which implied that he would even contemplate conversion.*
>
> *The bishop was beside himself with rage. Unable to control his wrath, he ordered that R' Amnon's legs be amputated since they had not carried him to the*

bishop after the three days. Then, R' Amnon's arms were likewise cut off. The bishop repeatedly berated R' Amnon and demanded, "Are you prepared to convert?" R' Amnon was steadfast in his refusal and the bishop sent him home in his mutilated condition.

When Rosh Hashanah arrived, R' Amnon was borne to the shul, where he asked to be placed in front of the Ark. Prior to the recitation of Kedushah, he said the Nesaneh Tokef prayer and then expired.

Shortly thereafter, R' Amnon appeared to R' Klonimus — a great kabbalist — and requested that his prayer, Unesaneh Tokef, become part of the Rosh Hashanah Mussaf liturgy and be recited by Jews everywhere and for all time.

וְיִכּוֹן בְּחֶסֶד כִּסְאֶךָ

Your throne will be firmed with kindness ...

The psalmist says "Your throne was firmed from of old" (*Psalms* 93:2). The Hebrew for "from of old" is *me'az,* and the Midrash compares the word *me'az* to the first word of the Song of Triumph upon the Splitting of the Reed Sea (*Exodus* 15:1), "*Az yashir.*" The miracle of the Splitting of the Reed Sea is described as a *chesed,* "With Your kindness You guided this people that You redeemed ..." (ibid. 15:13).

Hashem's *chesed* is constant (see *Psalms* 52:3), but it is not always acknowledged. Hence, Hashem's sovereignty is not always appreciated. When the Israelites sang *Az yashir,* in praise of Hashem's *chesed* at their deliverance, Hashem's throne was firmed.

This leads into the second phrase,

וְתֵשֵׁב עָלָיו בֶּאֱמֶת
... and You will sit upon it in truth.

*R' Levi Yitzchak of Berditchev said, "Master of the
universe! Truth is what is everlasting. If Your decrees
are with chesed, they will prevail forever. However, if
Your decrees will be with din, tzaddikim may overturn
them, as You have given them the ability to do so [Moed
Katan 16b], and since they will not endure, they will
not be in truth."*

וְכוֹתֵב וְחוֹתֵם
... Who writes and seals ....

*R' Levi Yitzchak of Berditchev cited the Mishnah
(Rosh Hashanah 4:1), "Yom Tov shel Rosh Hashanah
shechal beShabbos (When the festival of Rosh Hashanah
occurs on Shabbos), and translated it literally. "'It is
a good day when Rosh Hashanah occurs on Shabbos,'
because it is forbidden to write on Shabbos. However, in
case of pikuach nefesh [to save a life], one may write on
Shabbos. Therefore, Hashem will write only favorable
decrees for life when Rosh Hashanah occurs on Shabbos.
It is indeed a good day."*

וּבְשׁוֹפָר גָּדוֹל יִתָּקַע, וְקוֹל דְּמָמָה דַקָּה
***The great shofar will be sounded, and a still,
thin sound ...***

The Rebbe of Kotzk asked his student, R' Yechiel
Meir of Gostanin, to blow the shofar. However, R'
Yechiel Meir could manage to force only feeble sounds
from the shofar. After the davening, R' Yechiel Meir
apologized for his poor performance, but the Rebbe
said, "The verse can also be read, 'U'va shofar — and
with a shofar, gadol yitaka — a great person will blow,'
then, even though there may only be a still, thin sound,
nevertheless, this will cause the angels to tremble."

וְקוֹל דְּמָמָה דַקָּה יִשָּׁמַע
A still, thin sound will be heard.

We noted the meaning that Rav Saadiah Gaon and Rambam
ascribed to the shofar; namely, to arouse a person from lethargy. We
may be so preoccupied with the events of daily life that we pay little
attention to our spiritual needs. However, the *neshamah* within us
cannot be totally subdued. It makes itself heard, if only by a small,
still sound, telling us that we cannot be derelict in becoming the
spiritual beings we were meant to be. It is a still, thin sound, but
one that we cannot silence.

וּמַלְאָכִים יֵחָפֵזוּן
Angels will hasten....

Why will the angels hasten? The Talmud says that when a
person performs a mitzvah, a benevolent angel is created (*Ethics
of the Fathers* 4:13). The angel resulting from the mitzvah has
the characteristics of the mitzvah. If the mitzvah was performed

appropriately, with the proper *kavannah*, the angel is handsome and well formed. If the mitzvah was not done properly, the angel is deformed.

Many mitzvos are done in haste and with inadequate *kavannah*. When the angels resulting from these mitzvos pass before the Heavenly Tribunal, they do not want their defects to be noticed, so they hasten past (*Devash Vechalav*).

וְחִיל וּרְעָדָה יֹאחֵזוּן

A trembling and terror will seize them [the angels].

Even the heavenly angels are not free from being judged. "… He cannot have faith even in His servants and finds fault with His angels" (*Job* 4:18). As was noted, Hashem does not contravene His laws of justice. In order to give His beloved children, Israel, a favorable judgment, Hashem seeks to disqualify the accusing angels as valid witnesses to man's deeds.

וְכָל בָּאֵי עוֹלָם יַעַבְרוּן לְפָנֶיךָ כִּבְנֵי מָרוֹן

All mankind will pass before You like members of the flock.

After this statement, the Talmud continues, "And all are examined with one glance" (*Rosh Hashanah* 18a). If each person's actions are judged individually, one may indeed be subject to a harsh judgment.

When Abraham pleaded for the sinful people of Sodom, he said, "Will You also stamp out the righteous along with the wicked? … It would be sacrilege to You to do such a thing, to bring death upon the righteous along with the wicked …" (*Genesis* 18:23-25). *Bnei*

Yisaschar asks why Abraham would presume that Hashem would punish the righteous along with the wicked. He answers that even if a person is sinful, if he is compared to his peers who are worse sinners than he, he should be considered relatively righteous. This was Abraham's argument. "Will you punish the righteous along with the wicked?" — i.e., those who are relatively righteous when compared with the truly wicked.

In order to justify a lenient judgment for Israel, Hashem looks at all mankind with one glance. When we are compared to other nations, we are indeed righteous.

On Rosh Hashanah, Hashem implements His mercy by judging "all mankind with a single glance." When viewed in context of all the nations, there can be no doubt; we are still the finest in the world.

☞ *On Rosh Hashanah will be inscribed …*

מִי יִחְיֶה וּמִי יָמוּת
Who will live, and who will die...

There are numerous instances when one can see *Hashgachah Pratis* (Divine Providence) in operation, as in the case of the young man who inadvertently left his *tefillin* in the airport terminal. He begged to be let off to retrieve them, but was told that once the plane's door was closed, it was impossible to allow him to leave. He protested so vehemently that he was allowed to deplane, but he was not allowed to board again. That plane was one of the two that struck the World Trade Center on 9/11.

Stories of such "coincidences" abound. It has been wisely said that "coincidences are really miracles in which God chose to remain anonymous."

מִי בְקִצּוֹ וּמִי לֹא בְקִצּוֹ

*... who will die at his predestined time,
and who not at his time*

Why would a person die before his predestined time? This *piyut* may be following the opinion of the *Ohr HaChaim*. The Torah states that Reuben tried to save Joseph from his brothers' plan to kill him by throwing him into a pit (*Genesis* 37:22). However, the Talmud says that there were poisonous snakes in that pit, which would surely cause his death. *Ohr HaChaim* says that Reuben knew that Joseph was a *tzaddik* and would not be harmed by the snakes. However, the brothers were free agents, and inasmuch as Hashem does not intervene to stop a person from committing a crime, his being a *tzaddik* would not protect him from his brothers' actions. Thus, it is possible for a person to die at the hands of another person before his time.

> *There may be people who live beyond their predestined time. A man visited the Vilna Gaon in the latter's succah. The Gaon was so engrossed in his learning that he did not notice the man, who waited for a while and left. The man later asked the Gaon, "Why did you ignore me in the succah?"*
>
> *The Gaon apologized, "My dear man, please forgive me. I'm so sorry; I just did not see you. Hashem should bless you to live to be one hundred."*
>
> *When the man was ninety-eight, he became sick, and*

the family called a doctor. The man refused to be seen by the doctor. "I will recover," he said. "It is not my time to die. The Gaon said I would live to one hundred."

Indeed, the man died on his one hundredth birthday. Thus, a person may live beyond one's destined time as a result of a berachah.

וּתְשׁוּבָה וּתְפִלָּה וּצְדָקָה מַעֲבִירִין אֶת רֹעַ הַגְּזֵרה

But repentance, prayer, and tzedakah remove the evil of the decree!

How do these actions annul a harsh decree? Obviously, we cannot make Hashem change His mind.

One answer is that the decrees are issued on a conditional basis; i.e., thus and so will happen to a person unless he repents, prays, and gives *tzedakah*.

Rambam says that the reason *teshuvah* repeals a decree is because a person undergoes a character change by doing *teshuvah*, so that he is no longer the same person who committed the sin, and B cannot be punished for something that A did (*Laws of Teshuvah* 2:4). This is equally true of sincere prayer, which brings about a significant change in a person.

But how do prayers work for others? If Chaim prays for Yaakov to recover, why is his prayer effective for Yaakov?

R' Elimelech of Lizhensk says that if there was a decree that Yaakov should suffer, but Chaim cares deeply for Yaakov, then Yaakov's illness causes Chaim grief. However, Chaim is not deserving of distress. Therefore, to eliminate Chaim's anxiety, Yaakov is permitted to recover.

The word *tzedakah* was transliterated rather than translated as "charity," because the Torah concept is that *tzedakah* is not charity, Rather, in His infinite wisdom, Hashem gave much money to some people and little money to others, with the understanding that the money destined for the poor was given to the rich for safekeeping, and they are to distribute to the poor what is justly their portion.

Tzedakah is derived from the word *tzedek* (justice), and what one gives to the poor is justly theirs.

> *The Tzaddik of Sanz gave every cent he had to the poor. When his son told him that halachah provides that one should give no more than 20 percent for tzedakah, the Tzaddik said, "How can a child be so inconsiderate to his father? Every mitzvah has a shiur, a fixed amount to fulfill that mitzvah. For example, the shiur of matzah one is required to eat on Passover is a kezayis, equivalent to the size of an olive. The mitzvah of tzedakah, too, has a shiur, that of 20 percent. But in addition to the mitzvah of tzedakah, tzedakah also has the ability to attain forgiveness for one's sins. What would a person not give to save his life? I give tzedakah to save myself from the punishment for the many sins I have committed, and you wish to deny me this?"*

> *The Tzaddik used a glass beaker for the Seder, because his silver goblet had been pawned for tzedakah money to be given to the poor. One Erev Passover, when it was near sundown, he sent a messenger to a*

wealthy man asking him to lend him some money. The man complied, but wondered what the Tzaddik could possibly do with the money so close to the beginning of Yom Tov. The rich man knew that the Tzaddik had given tzedakah lavishly before the festival, and besides, all the stores had already closed and one could not buy anything at that point. Curious, he accompanied the messenger and asked the Tzaddik what he was going to do with the money.

The Tzaddik explained, "There is a merchant in town who has fallen on hard times and has become bankrupt. His creditors are hounding him for payment of his debts. How is he to have simchah on Yom Tov when he knows that right after the holiday he will be pressured for money? That is why I am giving him money now, late in the day, when it cannot be spent. He will have peace of mind knowing that he will have something to give his creditors after Yom Tov.

"Do you think tzedakah is limited to giving money for food and clothes? One must think of the other needs a person may have. This man has a need for simchas Yom Tov, and that, too, is tzedakah."

☞ *Easy to Appease*

אֱמֶת כִּי אַתָּה הוּא יוֹצְרָם, וְאַתָּה יוֹדֵעַ יִצְרָם
It is true that You are their Creator and You know their inclination (yitzram)...

In our defense, we enter the plea that Hashem created the *yetzer hara*, and actually expressed regret at having done so. A remarkable Midrash states: Three things Hashem regretted having created: the kingdom of Kasdim, the Ishmaelites, and the *yetzer hara* (*Midrash HaGadol Noach* 8:21).

It is difficult to take this message at face value, because Hashem does not regret His actions. This is a human fable. Nonetheless, these words do afford us some latitude.

אָדָם יְסוֹדוֹ מֵעָפָר
A man's origin is from dust ...

This concept is also mentioned in the *Avinu Malkeinu*. "Our Father, Our King, remember that we are but dust."

Oheiv Yisrael cites *Rashi*, who states that Hashem commanded the earth to produce a tree with bark and branches that would have the same taste of the fruit it bears, but the earth disobeyed and produced a tree that indeed bore fruit, but the tree itself did not have the taste of the fruit. Therefore, when man was punished for his sin, the earth was punished for its sin (*Genesis* 1:11).

The concept that the earth could sin is generally explained as referring to the angel that Hashem assigned as custodian of the earth. But why would this angel disobey Hashem's command? An angel does not have a *yetzer hara* that tempts it to sin. Furthermore, why was the earth's punishment postponed until man sinned?

Oheiv Yisrael explains that the earth's angel knew that man was destined to sin. Therefore, to mitigate man's sin, the earth intentionally disobeyed Hashem's command so that man could defend himself by saying, "I'm not to blame entirely. After all, I was made of a substance that sinned, so I am innately prone to sin." When man eventually sinned, the earth was punished because it had contributed to his sin.

So, on Rosh Hashanah we ask Hashem to be merciful with us. "Our Father, Our King, remember that we are but dust." You created us of a substance that had sinned.

> *In a lighter vein, a man was noted to be crying during the prayers. "Why are you crying?" he was asked. He pointed to the text, "Look how tragic man is, made of dust and returns to dust."*
>
> *Someone said to him, "That's tragic? If he were made of gold and turns to dust, that would be tragic. But if he is made of dust and returns to dust, and in between can make a l'chaim, why, that's all profit!"*

בְּנַפְשׁוֹ יָבִיא לַחְמוֹ

... at the risk of his life he earns his bread.

One of the tzaddikim challenged the Satan. "How dare you bring charges against us to Hashem! You are up in heaven and are free of worries. You do not have a family to support. You have never lost a job and worried how you will pay your children's tuition. You have never spent a sleepless night caring for a sick infant. You have never had to brave a blizzard and subzero weather to obtain medicine for a sick child. You have never been threatened with foreclosure on your home. You have no stresses, so you are free to search for mistakes people have made. Come down to earth and endure the stresses we humans have, and we'll see how perfect you are!"

When we ask forgiveness for our sins, we ask Hashem to consider the pressures under which we live, and to disregard the contentions of the Satan.

מָשׁוּל כְּחֶרֶס הַנִּשְׁבָּר, כֶּחָצִיר יָבֵשׁ

He (man) is likened to a broken shard, withering grass ...

What is the purpose of seeing oneself as a broken shard or withering grass? The Maggid of Dubnow related a parable.

> *There was a very wise man who was very poor. He approached a wealthy man and said, "I know that I am very knowledgeable. I just haven't had any mazal. If I could enter into a partnership with you, I could advise you how to make more money."*
>
> *The wealthy man said, "Why do I need you as a partner? My investments are doing well."*
>
> *The wise man said, "I'm not suggesting a 50-50 partnership. I will take only 10 percent. Give me this chance. I will show you it will be profitable." The wealthy man agreed to this.*
>
> *The results of the partnership were indeed gainful, and the 10 percent brought the wise man a fair amount of money. He could now buy good food and nice clothing.*
>
> *After a while, the wise man's wife, who had become accustomed to a more affluent lifestyle, began nagging*

him. "You are a partner in his business, yet he drives a luxury car and goes on expensive cruises, while we have an inexpensive car and we don't go anywhere."

The wise man could not withstand her nagging. He approached the wealthy man, saying, "I want to dissolve our partnership."

"Why do you want to do that? We're doing so well."

The wise man said, "I really don't want to dissolve the partnership, but I want to show my wife, as clearly as possible, that I have only a 10 percent interest in the business and don't need anymore."

The Maggid said, "We have many of the goods of this world, but our appetites are insatiable. We think we deserve more than we have, the luxuries that others have. We are told to remember that we are like a broken shard and withering grass. We have been provided with only a small fraction of this world."

☞ *The Living and Enduring God.*

מָשׁוּל כְּחֶרֶס הַנִּשְׁבָּר ... וּכְרוּחַ נוֹשָׁבֶת, וּכְאָבָק פּוֹרֵחַ, וְכַחֲלוֹם יָעוּף

He [man] is likened to a broken shard, withering grass, a fading flower, a passing shade, a dissipating cloud, a blowing wind, flying dust, and a fleeting dream.

וְאַתָּה הוּא מֶלֶךְ אֵל חַי וְקַיָּם

But You are the King, the living and enduring God.

The above *piyut* presents a contrast that has no parallel. On the one hand stands man, with his absolute frailty and nothingness, and on the other hand we find Hashem, eternal, infinite, and omnipotent.

> *R' Naftali of Ropshitz said that a person should have two pockets, In one he should place a slip of paper reading, "Be exceedingly humble" (Ethics of the Fathers 4:4), and in the other, a slip of paper reading, "A person is obligated to say, 'The world was created for me'" (Sanhedrin 37a). At times a person should reach into one pocket, at other times into the other pocket.*

The *Book of Koheles* goes to great lengths to describe man's lowly status. "Futility of futility, all is futile." There is no lasting substance to any human endeavor. Indeed, man is like a broken shard and all the other totally insignificant things the lyricist lists. But, we must remember, "Beloved is man, for he was created in God's image" (*Ethics of the Fathers* 3:18). We have within us a *neshamah* that is of Divine origin, and we share in Hashem's eternity, infinity, and omnipotence.

R' Chaim Shmulevitz cites the Midrash on the verse "You shall be holy" (*Leviticus* 19:2) upon which the Midrash comments, "You might think that you can be as holy as Hashem is, therefore, the Torah says, 'for holy am I,' i.e., My holiness is superior to yours." Think of it! A mere mortal might think that he could equal the holiness of Hashem! That is because the *neshamah* within us is part of Hashem (*Sichos Mussar* 5731:18).

We are at one and the same time absolute nothingness, but by virtue of our *neshamah* and being connected to Hashem, we are also infinitely great.

Great Torah personalities were able to steer a course between

these two poles. Moses was the prototypical *anav*, the most
humble person on the face of the earth (*Numbers* 12:3), but
when necessary, as with the rebellion of Korah, he asserted his
authority.

Most people need to focus on *anivus* (humility).

> *Chida writes that in the days of the Maharshal (R'*
> *Shlomo Luria) there was a vegetable store located on the*
> *first floor of a building, beneath the beis midrash on an*
> *upper story. The proprietor, a man named Avraham,*
> *was apparently a simple, unlearned person. One late*
> *night, Maharshal heard R' Avraham learning Talmud*
> *aloud, with brilliant interpretation of a difficult*
> *portion of the Talmud.*
>
> *Maharshal sent a messenger to consult R' Avraham*
> *about a difficult halachic problem, but R' Avraham*
> *said that he had no knowledge about such things.*
> *Maharshal then confronted R' Avraham himself,*
> *ordering him, by his authority as mara d'asra (rabbi of*
> *the community) to respond. It was evident that he was*
> *an outstanding Torah scholar. R' Avraham pleaded*
> *with Maharshal not to disclose the truth about him.*
> *Unbeknownst to everyone, Maharshal and R' Avraham*
> *studied Torah together.*
>
> *Before his death, Maharshal instructed the*
> *community that R' Avraham, the proprietor of the*
> *vegetable store, should succeed him as rabbi of the*
> *community because he was a Torah giant. Only with*
> *intense pleadings did R' Avraham finally consent*

to serve as the community's spiritual leader (*Shem HaGedolim A, p. 76*).
   That is anivus.

The *sifrei mussar* are replete with the great spiritual value of *anivus*, teaching us that Hashem responds readily to the prayers of an *anav*. It is especially important in our Rosh Hashanah prayers that we pray in a state of *anivus*.

אֵין קִצְבָה לִשְׁנוֹתֶיךָ

There Is No Set Span to Your Years

This *piyut* lauds the eternity of Hashem and His infinite glory, and states that Hashem has given us the privilege of identifying with Him: And You have included Your Name in our name.

This *piyut* is sung with a cheerful, moving melody, often accompanied by the congregants clapping their hands to the beat.

Baba Beilish was the daughter of R' Eliezer of Dzhikov. My grandmother remembered her well, and related this story to us.

> *R' Eliezer had fallen seriously ill, and the Tzaddik of Sanz came to visit him. Baba Beilish overheard this conversation.*
>
> *R' Eliezer wept and said, "Holy mechuten, pray that I get well."*
>
> *The Tzaddik said, "Mechuten, you know what bliss awaits you in the Next World. Why are you so insistent on staying in this earthly world?"*
>
> *R' Eliezer said, "But who will support my family if I die?"*

The Tzaddik said, "I assure you that I will take care of all their needs."

R' Eliezer said, "But mechuten, we are just a few weeks away from Rosh Hashanah. You know that when I sing 'Ain Kitzvah,' the heavenly angels join in the song."

The Tzaddik said, "In that case, have the mikveh warmed up for me."

After emerging from the mikveh and concluding his prayers, the Tzaddik was elated. "I succeeded in keeping him with us."

R' Eliezer lived for an additional six years.

בְּאֵין מֵלִיץ יֹשֶׁר
In the Absence of an Advocate

The words of the *machzor* are translated as follows: In the absence of an advocate against the one who reports transgression [the Satan], may You testify for the sake of Jacob['s offspring] regarding [their observance of Your] decrees and ordinances, thereby may You vindicate us in the judgment, O King of judgment.

For the meaning of this *piyut*, it is necessary to focus on the Hebrew word for decree, *chok*.

The mitzvos are divided into three categories: *eidus*, pertaining to commemorating events, such as the festivals; *mishpatim*, societal laws; and *chukim*, laws for which no logical reason is given, such as *shaatnez*, the prohibition of wearing a mixture of linen and wool. Whereas we may understand why we observe *eidus* and *mishpatim,* the *chukim* are observed on blind faith, solely because Hashem decreed them.

R' Levi Yitzchak of Berditchev explained the above *piyut* as an argument. "If we have no advocate to defend us against the charges brought against us by the Satan, and there is no logical reason to grant us forgiveness, then we ask You, Hashem, to invoke in our behalf the merit of the fact that we observed *chukim,* mitzvos that have no logic. We, therefore, should be forgiven even if there is no logic to it."

> *R' Moshe Leib of Sasov also explained the above piyut, focusing on the word "mishpat," the halachah of trial law. "Master if the universe!" he said. "If we do not have an advocate to defend us, then we request that You apply the Torah mishpatim, as follows:*
>
> *"1. The defendant has the right to face the accuser. Our trial in heaven is being held in our absence, and we do not have the opportunity to answer the charges.*
>
> *"2. Rambam says that only someone who has raised children and has developed compassion is qualified to act as a judge. The judges of the Heavenly Tribunal do not meet this qualification.*
>
> *"3. A witness must be capable of being impeached. None of those who testify against us are able to be impeached.*
>
> *"4. The Satan incites people to sin, hence he is a criminal, and that disqualifies him to be a witness against us.*
>
> *"5. The halachah is that the plaintiff must go to the*

court of the defendant, so the accuser must present his charges in a court of human judges.

"Thus, Master of the universe! Since we have no advocate to defend us, we ask that You invoke Torah law and declare the trial invalid."

ᐸ *True Emunah*

וְכֹל מַאֲמִינִים
All believe

The Midrash says that the only *zechus* (merit) for *parnassah* (sustenance) is *emunah* (see Rashi, *Psalms* 37:3).

We are told that we will receive reward for mitzvos in Gan Eden, not in this world. The commentaries ask: Inasmuch as Hashem abides by all the laws of the Torah, and the Torah says that one may not postpone the payment of a laborer, how can Hashem postpone the reward for our mitzvos? They answer that the halachah is that if one hired laborers via an agent, he is not bound by the requirement to pay on the same day. Inasmuch as Moses was Hashem's agent in commanding the mitzvos, the payment may be postponed until Gan Eden.

However, the first two of the Ten Commandments, which are the mitzvah of *emunah*, were given to us directly by Hashem, not via Moses (*Makkos* 24a). Therefore, observing the mitzvah of *emunah* entitles us to immediate reward in this world. Hence, the only *zechus* for *parnassah* is *emunah*, because this mitzvah was given to us directly, not via an agent.

הַטּוֹב, וּמֵטִיב לָרָעִים וְלַטּוֹבִים
Who is good, and benefits the wicked and the good

Why are the wicked cited before the good?

The Torah says, "He shall not delay for His enemy — in his lifetime He shall repay him" (*Deuteronomy* 7:10). Rashi explains that a *rasha* (wicked person) is rewarded in this world for whatever mitzvos he may have done and he comes empty-handed to Gan Eden, whereas the righteous person receives his reward in Gan Eden. Thus, the wicked are rewarded before the good.

> *A profligate sinner said to R' Levi Yitzchak of Berditchev, "You say I will be punished for my sins? Look at me. I am healthy and wealthy and I enjoy life."*
>
> *R' Levi Yitzchak said, "How would you know that you would be punished for your sins? You must have come across that in the Shema. My dear child, if you said the Shema only once, there is not enough money in the world to reward you for that."*

R' Hirsch of Zidachov interpreted the above phrase as "to those who think they are sinful, and to those who think they are righteous."

The Baal Shem Tov said, "I prefer a *rasha* who knows that he is a *rasha* to a *tzaddik* who knows he is a *tzaddik*. Anyone who thinks himself to be a *tzaddik* is haughty, someone whom Hashem cannot tolerate. Those who think of themselves as sinful are more virtuous than those who think themselves to be righteous."

> *The Rebbe of Apt said, "No one ever got the better of me, except one individual.*
>
> *"This person came to ask my advice. I could tell that the individual was very sinful, and I said, 'You have the insolence to step into this holy house?'*
>
> *"The reply was, 'Hashem has patience with the wicked. He is in no hurry to make them pay their debts, and He does not attack them, lest they be ashamed to turn to Him. But the Rebbe of Apt sits there in his chair and cannot resist revealing what Hashem has left concealed!'"*

Indeed, Hashem benefits the wicked and the good.

וְכֹל מַאֲמִינִים שֶׁהוּא יוֹצְרָם בַּבָּטֶן

All believe that He fashioned them from the womb.

It is beyond me how any thinking person can deny the existence of God.

A physician said, "I was peering through the microscope at a single cell invisible to the naked eye, and it struck me that from now on, all this cell will receive is the elements carbon, oxygen, hydrogen, nitrogen, and a few trace metals, and from them it will fashion a full human being that can see, hear, speak, and think. I then realized that there must be a God."

We see people around us all the time, so we do not think of them as miraculous creatures. Yet, a human being has a brain with *one hundred billion* neurons (functioning) cells with even more supportive cells. Each neuron connects with up to 10,000 other neurons, functioning in mind-staggering precision. Add to this the unbelievable functioning of the liver, kidney, heart, and other organs, and all of this is accomplished by a tiny, microscopic cell using only carbon, oxygen, hydrogen, nitrogen, and a few trace metals! It takes greater effort to deny God than it does to believe in Him.

הַפּוֹתֵחַ שַׁעַר לְדוֹפְקֵי בִתְשׁוּבָה

Who opens a gate to those who knock in repentance.

As previously noted, the Midrash quotes Hashem as saying, "Open for Me a portal of *teshuvah* as tiny as the point of a needle, and I will open for you doors through which wagons and coaches can enter" (*Shir HaShirim Rabbah* 5:3). All that is required is that a person makes a sincere effort at *teshuvah*, and Hashem will help him the rest of the way.

The Rebbe of Kotzk says, "Yes, a portal of *teshuvah* as tiny as the point of a needle may be adequate, but it must penetrate through and through."

As mentioned above, the Talmud cites the case of Elazar ben Doradia, who was a profligate sinner all his life; when he realized his error, he began crying bitterly in *teshuvah*. He cried so incessantly that he died while crying, and a heavenly voice proclaimed that his *teshuvah* had been accepted (*Avodah Zarah* 17a). That is what the Rebbe of Kotzk meant: The needle point of *teshuvah* must penetrate through and through.

During the *chazzan's* repetition the shofar is sounded in each of the segments of *Malchios, Zichronos,* and *Shofros.* Immediately after each set of shofar blasts the following is recited.

הַיוֹם הֲרַת עוֹלָם הַיוֹם יַעֲמִיד בַּמִּשְׁפָּט כָּל יְצוּרֵי עוֹלָמִים, אִם כְּבָנִים, אִם
כַּעֲבָדִים. אִם כְּבָנִים, רַחֲמֵנוּ כְּרַחֵם אָב עַל בָּנִים, וְאִם כַּעֲבָדִים עֵינֵינוּ לְךָ
תְלוּיוֹת, עַד שֶׁתְּחָנֵּנוּ וְתוֹצִיא כָאוֹר מִשְׁפָּטֵנוּ, אָיוֹם קָדוֹשׁ.

*Today is the birth[day] of the world. Today all creatures
of the world stand in judgment — whether as children [of
God] or as servants. If as children, be merciful with us as the
mercy of a father for children. If as servants, our eyes [look
toward and] depend upon You, until You will be gracious to
us and release our verdict [clear and pure] as light,
O Awesome and Holy One.*

We are always dependent on Hashem, even when we are as children. The verse seems to imply that we are dependent on Hashem only when we are as servants.

The key is in the words "be gracious." Grace connotes a gift that the person did not earn. When we are obedient to Hashem and have a loving relationship with Him as children to their father, we know He will be merciful to us, and we do not have to plead for grace. Servants do not have this relationship, and they do what their master orders because they have no choice. If we serve Hashem only out of fear of punishment for violating the Torah's commandments, we are as servants and cannot expect that He relate to us with the feelings of a father for a child. We can only hope that He will be gracious to us.

Bnei Yisaschar cites the Talmud passage stating that when we do Hashem's will, we are considered His children. If we do not do His will, we are considered His servants (*Shemos Rabbah* 24:1).

If we are judged only as His servants rather than His children, we may not receive a favorable judgment.

During the reign of Herod, one of his slaves killed someone and was brought to trial before the Sanhedrin. Shimon ben Shatach, the chief justice of the Sanhedrin, sent for Herod to come to the trial because he owned the slave, and thus he, Herod, was essentially the defendant. Herod came, and Shimon ben Shatach told him that the halachah requires that he must stand while the testimony is given, but Herod, as ruler of the land, refused.

If we are brought to trial on Rosh Hashanah and we are in the position of being Hashem's servants, then as our Master, He would have to stand to hear the testimony against us. But it is impossible to order the King of Glory to stand.

Thus we say, "If as servants, our eyes [look toward and] depend upon You, our Master, to be at the trial with us." Inasmuch as the halachah that the master must stand cannot be fulfilled, the trial cannot go on and the case against us must be dismissed.

The Maggid of Dubnow commented on the above *piyut* with a parable.

> *A man had a wayward son, and when he could no longer tolerate the boy's behavior, the father ordered him to leave the house. The lad met some young men in the street and joined them. They welcomed him, but told him he would have to contribute to the group's expenses. Since the lad had no money, he went from door to door asking for handouts. Eventually, he knocked on the door of his own home. When the father answered the door, he said, "Get out of here! I told you I did not want you in this house."*

The lad said, "You are right, Father, but you give to every beggar who knocks on your door, irrespective of his behavior. Why am I any worse than a stranger?"

Therefore we say, "If we haven't been behaving as You want us to as Your children, please be kind to us as You are to strangers."

☞ *Accept With Mercy*

אֲרֶשֶׁת שְׂפָתֵינוּ
May the Utterance of Our Lips

May the utterance of our lips be pleasant before You, O exalted and uplifted God, Who discerns and gives ear, looks closely and hearkens, to the sound of our shofar blasts, and may You accept with mercy and favor the order of our Kingship verses.

In addition to *Today is the birth[day] of the world*, this *piyut* is repeated after each sounding of the shofar in the *Amidah*.

We ask Hashem to accept our prayers by virtue of our sounding the shofar. In what way does the shofar make our prayers more effective?

Following the *Shofros* verses, we recite the *berachah*, "Blessed are You, Hashem, Who hears the shofar-sound of His people Israel with mercy."

On Yom Kippur, we recite the *berachah*, "Blessed are You, Hashem, the King Who pardons and forgives our iniquities and the iniquities of His people, the family of Israel, and removes our sins every single year."

R' Levi Yitzchak of Berditchev related a parable of the
children at cheder. One child brought some cookies, and
another child asked him for a cookie, but the former
refused to give it to him. The second child then recited
the berachah "borei minei mezonos," which is said for
eating pastries. If one recites the berachah but does not
eat, he will have pronounced the Name of Hashem in
vain, which is a sin. He knew that his friend would not
allow him to have sinned, so he had to give him a cookie.

"This," said R' Levi Yitzchak, "is what we do. We recite the *berachah*, 'Blessed are You, Hashem, the King Who pardons and forgives our iniquities and the iniquities of His people, the family of Israel, and removes our sins every single year.' If Hashem does not forgive us, we will have recited the *berachah* in vain, which Hashem would not allow. Thus, Hashem is compelled, so to speak, to forgive our sins."

Here, too, we apply the same strategy. We recite the *berachah*, "Blessed are You, Hashem, Who hears the shofar-sound of His people Israel with mercy." In order that this not be a *berachah* recited in vain, Hashem must, so to speak, accept the shofar-sounds with mercy.

Please allow me to share with you one of my favorite childhood memories.

At a very young age, I learned how to blow shofar,
and my father gave me my own little shofar. One Rosh
Hashanah, after my older brother had blown the first set
of sounds, he went to a nearby shul to blow shofar for that
congregation. It is our custom to blow the shofar during

*the silent Amidah, and a congregant was designated
to do so. However, regardless of how much he tried, no
sound came out of his shofar.*

*The shofar was passed around to several worshipers,
but with no luck. I figured that it was time for me to
act, so I blew the sounds on my little shofar. Each man
had covered his head with his tallis, as is usual during
shofar-blowing, so no one knew who had blown the
shofar. When it was later discovered that the shofar
had been blown by a minor, which did not fulfill the
mitzvah, all the sounds had to be blown again when my
brother returned.*

*My father never tired telling people about my stunt.
(From* Gevurah — My Life, Our World, and the
Adventure of Reaching 80)

☞ Cling to Hashem

וְנֶאֱמַר: ... וְאַתֶּם הַדְּבֵקִים בַּה' אֱלֹקֵיכֶם, חַיִּים כֻּלְּכֶם הַיּוֹם

*And it is said ... "You, who cling to Hashem, your God,
you are all alive today" (Deuteronomy 4:4).*

The Talmud says, "How can a person cling to Hashem? By
clinging to His *middos*. Just as He is merciful, so should you be
merciful. Just as He is compassionate, so should you be compassionate" (*Sotah* 14a).

> *The Maggid of Dubnow related a parable about a great
> Torah scholar whose son was not the brightest student.*

— 224 —

*The youth was able to grasp only the superficial text
of the Talmud, but was unable to analyze it in depth.
The father, who had written prolifically on Talmudic
analysis, gave his son some of his writings, in the hope
that this would motivate the son to intensify his study of
the Talmud.*

*After several months, the father asked his son what he
thought of his writings. The son said, "Father, you sure
are a genius."*

*The father was disappointed. He had hoped that the
son would emulate his Talmudic study. His intention
was not to be told that he was a genius.*

So we pray on Rosh Hashanah, extolling the greatness of
Hashem. But that is not the point. Hashem wants us to emulate
His attributes with which we praise Him. That way, we will be
clinging to Hashem, and we will earn a favorable judgment.

☞ *Strengthen Us*

הַיּוֹם תְּאַמְּצֵנוּ
Today May You Strengthen Us

The Ark is opened when this segment is recited.

The Hebrew may also be translated, "Today, You *will* strengthen
us," a statement of confidence that Hashem will indeed bless us
with a good year.

Let me reiterate what was said earlier.

These truly are indeed solemn and awesome days, but they are nevertheless festivals, days when we should have *simchah*, confident that a loving Father in Heaven will bless us with all that is good. After chastising the people on Rosh Hashanah for their waywardness, the prophet Nehemiah said, "Do not mourn and do not weep …. Eat rich foods and drink sweet beverages, and send portions to those who have nothing prepared, for today is sacred to our Lord. Do not be sad; the enjoyment of Hashem is your strength" (*Nehemiah* 8:9-10).

Tashlich

*I*t is customary, on Rosh Hashanah afternoon (if the first day of Rosh Hashanah is Shabbos, this is done on the second day), to perform the ritual of *Tashlich*. If one cannot do so in the second day, he is permitted to perform *Tashlich* at any time until Yom Kippur. There are opinions that *Tashlich* may be said even until Hoshana Rabbah.

The word "*tashlich*" means "to cast away," hence there is a popular opinion that by this ritual, one casts one's sins into the water. This reasoning is immature. One cannot divest oneself of sins by throwing them into the water. Sins are removed only by sincere *teshuvah*.

What, then, is the purpose of *Tashlich*? Like other practices of Rosh Hashanah, such as eating certain foods and saying a special *yehi ratzon* (May it be Your will), *Tashlich* is a symbol that must be understood.

The reason most commonly cited for *Tashlich* is that it is similar to other references to the *Akeidah* (Binding of Isaac). The Midrash states that Satan used every possible maneuver to deter Abraham from following through with the *Akeidah*. Satan used his considerable powers to create an impassable river, but Abraham and Isaac forged the river, and when they were up to their necks in water, Abraham cried, "Save me, O God, for the waters have reached until the soul" (*Psalms* 69:2).

Sometimes we are faced with what seem to be formidable barriers to doing the will of Hashem. The teachings of the *Akeidah* are that we must persist, and the barriers will disappear,

There is another teaching derived from the dialogue between Abraham and the Satan. The Talmud says that the verse, "You shall love Hashem with all your heart" (*Deuteronomy* 6:5), means "with both the *yetzer tov* and the *yetzer hara*" (*Berachos* 54a). How are we to serve Hashem with the *yetzer hara*?

Chassidic writings say that when we see something beautiful or something that arouses an intense desire within us, we should reflect, "Whence did this object obtain such beauty or such an enticing nature? Why, from Hashem, of course. Then why should I be attracted to something that is only a derivative of Hashem, when I can be close to the source, to Hashem Himself?" In this way, the desire of the *yetzer hara* is put to a positive use.

This, too, happened to Abraham. Let us reflect. Abraham knew the entire Torah. He knew that human sacrifice was an abomination to Hashem. When he heard Hashem tell him to bring Isaac as an offering, an action that he knew to be against the Torah, why did he not consider, "Perhaps I am hallucinating. What I heard cannot possibly be the voice of Hashem. Hashem would never want this."

Although I do not have a source to verify this, I believe that Abraham *did* consider this, and he set out on the trip to Moriah with the thought that during the next three days he would be able to resolve whether this was indeed the voice of Hashem or a hallucination.

The Midrash says that the Satan encountered Abraham.

> *"Where are you going?" the Satan asked.*
>
> *Abraham responded, "We are just going for an outing."*
>
> *"Then why do you have a knife, wood, and fire?" Satan asked.*
>
> *Abraham answered, "Just in case we want to have meat, I'll slaughter a sheep."*
>
> *Satan said, "Old man, why are you lying to me? Don't you think I overheard when Hashem told you to sacrifice Isaac?"*
>
> *Abraham was overjoyed. "Now I know that it was indeed Hashem speaking to me and not a hallucination!" and he continued to the Akeidah with renewed vigor.*
>
> *Abraham had used the yetzer hara, the Satan, in the service of Hashem.*

The symbolism of going to a body of water that contains fish is because the eyes of fish are always open, and we are thus reminded that "[Hashem's] eyes are cognizant to all the ways of mankind" (*Jeremiah* 32:19).

Another symbolism found in *Tashlich* is that in Scriptural times it was customary to anoint the king at a river's edge. When we accept the sovereignty of Hashem on Rosh Hashanah, it is likened to attending His coronation, and we go to a body of water to emphasize this.

Among the prayers we recite in *Tashlich* is the verse "He will again be merciful to us; He will suppress our iniquities. And cast into the depths of the sea all their sins" (*Micah* 7:19). Some add the verse, "And all the sins of Your nation, the House of Israel, cast away to a place where they will neither be remembered, considered, nor brought to mind — ever."

Thus, *Tashlich* does not mean that we throw our sins into the water, but rather it is an assurance that when we do *teshuvah*, Hashem will cast away our sins and they will never be held against us. We cast away our sins, i.e., with *teshuvah*.

> *R' Naftali of Ropshitz was on his way to Tashlich and met the Seer of Lublin, who was returning from Tashlich.*
>
> *"Where are you going, Naftali?" the seer asked.*
> *R' Naftali answered, "I'm going to fetch the sins that the rebbe threw away!"*

Tzaddikim were very scrupulous about how they performed mitzvos, and they did *teshuvah* for their mitzvos, feeling that they did not do them with adequate perfection. What they considered imperfect would be a very high standard of perfection for us. R' Naftali said that he wished to have the "imperfect" mitzvos for which the Seer had done *teshuvah*.

Another water-related ritual is fetching water to bake matzah for Passover. The Talmud says that when one does *teshuvah* out of fear of Hashem, one's intentional sins are reduced to a status of unintentional sins. If one does *teshuvah* out of love for Hashem, the sins are converted into merits (*Yoma* 86b).

During the awesome days of Rosh Hashanah through Yom Kippur, our obligation to do *teshuvah* is basically discharged out of fear of Hashem. When we prepare for Passover to celebrate

Hashem's delivering us from Egypt, our love for Hashem converts our sins into merits. Therefore, we go to the water's edge to retrieve those sins that, through Hashem's acceptance of our sincere repentence, have now been transformed into merits.

Maintaining the Momentum

In the chapter on *zerizus* (diligence) in *Mesillas Yesharim*, Ramchal states that there are two necessary phases to diligence: (1) the enthusiasm at the initiation of a project, and (2) maintaining the enthusiasm as the project goes on. It is characteristic that one may have great enthusiasm at the initiation of a project, but it may gradually wane as the project progresses.

We may build up much enthusiasm on Rosh Hashanah, inspired by our awareness that Hashem is judging us and decreeing our fortune for the oncoming year. But as the holy days pass, we may fall into our previous routine, and our enthusiasm may dissipate. The failures of "New Year's resolutions" are common knowledge.

Let us recap. Rosh Hashanah commemorates the sixth day of creation, the day on which man was created. Animals and angels had already been created in a state of completion: animals completely physical creatures, under absolute domination of their bodily urges, and angels, completely spiritual creatures that have no desires other than to praise Hashem and carry out His wishes. Then came man, in every way an animal with powerful physical urges, but with a *neshamah* (soul) that enables him to be master over his bodily urges. Indeed, the

Vilna Gaon states that the entire purpose of man's creation is that he convert his physical drives to comply with Hashem's will.

This was Adam, nascent man on the sixth day of creation, and Rosh Hashanah recalls this day. Rosh Hashanah is a *yom hazikaron*, a day of remembrance not only in the sense that Hashem recalls our history, both as individuals and as humanity as a whole, but also a day on which *we* can recall the day of our creation.

Let me explain with an example from medicine. In the first few months of an infant's life, the child is given several injections in order to be immunized against a number of serious diseases. These injections cause the body to produce antibodies against these viruses and bacteria. A blood sample taken from the infant will reveal a high content of these antibodies. Over the years, the antibodies gradually dissipate so that at, say, age twenty, a blood sample will show barely a trace of these antibodies.

A person is then given a "booster shot," and the body promptly responds by producing a massive amount of antibodies, similar to that of the recently immunized infant. The body "remembers" what it must do, and the booster shot triggers its response to the injections of twenty years earlier.

Hayom haras olam. This is the day of the incipience of mankind. It is more than a commemoration of the past. It is *our yom hazikaron*. Our *neshamah* recalls the day of its instillation into the body of Adam, and we are brought back to the very moment of our creation, in which we are in a pure, pristine state of spirituality, with the ability to bring about the *olam hatikun*, the rectified world. Each of us is Adam, and it is our responsibility, as individuals as well as the whole, to bring about the perfection of the world. On Rosh Hashanah we should think of ourselves as Adam before his sin!

Yet another significance of Rosh Hashanah: *"Rosh"* means "head." The head holds the organs of vision, hearing, and smell, through which the brain gathers information that it processes to determine our behavior. Hashem forbade partaking of the Tree of Knowledge, but "the woman *saw* that the tree was good for eating and that it was a delight to the eyes" (*Genesis* 3:6). She *listened* to the words of the serpent that were contrary to the words of Hashem, and that resulted in Adam's and Eve's downfall.

In our personal *yom hazikaron*, when we are taken back to our creation, we are actually in the state of Adam and Eve *before their sin*. If we safeguard our eyes and ears to avoid exposure to that which Hashem has forbidden, we can prevent a downfall. Once we see and hear that which is contrary to Hashem's will, we are vulnerable to the seduction of the serpent, the *yetzer hara* within us.

Rosh Hashanah, in the sense of our personal creation, should inspire us to subject our own *"rosh"* to Hashem's sovereignty. Maintaining the *zerizus* of Rosh Hashanah requires reinforcement. We can accomplish this by consistent study of *Mesillas Yesharim* and similar works of *mussar*.

We can and should take this spirit of Rosh Hashanah with us throughout the year. We can see ourselves as pure and unblemished. We can accept the absolute sovereignty of Hashem. We can avoid replication of Adam's sin, of being lured by sensory attractions. We can use the unfettered abilities within our Divine *neshamah* to achieve our personal perfection, and thereby to contribute to *tikun olam*, perfection of the world.

Leshanah tovah tikaseiv veseichaseim. May you be inscribed and sealed for a good, sweet year.